Intersectional Theology

Intersectional Theology

An Introductory Guide

GRACE JI-SUN KIM AND SUSAN M. SHAW

FORTRESS PRESS
MINNEAPOLIS

INTERSECTIONAL THEOLOGY
An Introductory Guide

Copyright © 2018 Fortress Press. All rights reserved. Except for brief quotations in critical articles or reviews, no part of this book may be reproduced in any manner without prior written permission from the publisher. Email copyright@fortresspress.com or write to Permissions, Fortress Press, PO Box 1209, Minneapolis, MN 55440-1209.

Cover design: Joe Reinke

Print ISBN: 978-1-5064-4609-7
eBook ISBN: 978-1-5064-4610-3

To my loving daughter Elisabeth Sophia Lee, who truly embodies beauty, grace, and strength, and to my cousin Yoo Jin Hwang, for always surprising me with her kindness and understanding

—*Grace Ji-Sun Kim*

To OSU's Women, Gender, and Sexuality Studies faculty, who teach me every day what the work of justice and love looks like in practice. #WGSSLOVE

—*Susan M. Shaw*

Contents

	Acknowledgments	ix
	Preface	xi
1.	Introduction to Intersectionality	1
2.	Biography as Intersectional Theology	19
3.	Intersectionality as Theological Method	41
4.	Applying Intersectionality to Theology and the Bible	65
5.	Practicing Intersectional Theology	79
6.	Conclusion	107
	Glossary	113
	Bibliography	119
	Index	123

Acknowledgments

This book is the result of collaboration—but a collaboration greater than just the one between Grace and Susan. First we must begin by acknowledging the essential, deep, and complex work of black feminists who identified, named, and explicated intersectionality as a framework for understanding and analyzing their experiences of interlocking systems of oppression. Any work on intersectionality is indebted to their vision, wisdom, and scholarship.

We also appreciate the writings of the many scholars whose work centers intersectionality and challenges the church to transform itself toward inclusion, equity, and justice. We are part of a much longer story of contextual theologies, theologies of liberation, and struggles for justice.

We are grateful to the Reading and Support Group—Kryn Freehling-Burton, Amy Koehlinger, Vicki Tolar Burton, and Tara Williams—who read our manuscript and provided valuable feedback.

We also want to thank the editors at Fortress Press. We first thank Michael Gibson for believing in our project and understanding its importance. We also thank Will Bergkamp for assisting us in the transition period at Fortress Press, and our editor Paul Lutter for supporting our project and bringing this book to be.

Grace would like to thank her spouse, Perry Lee, for his continuous support in her various writing projects and in particular this book. She also thanks her three children, Theodore, Elisabeth, and Joshua, who are her biggest fans. She is always grateful for their continual understanding, kindness, and love when she is writing.

Susan thanks her spouse, Catherine Draper, for her support, understanding, cheerleading, and laughter while Susan's absorbed in writing, surrounded by piles of books, and oblivious to the rest of the world!

Preface

We met five years ago when Susan was teaching Grace's book *The Grace of Sophia* in her feminist theologies class. Grace came to Corvallis and spoke in the class, and we started talking about collaborating on a project together some day. We finally reached a moment in time when neither of us had a major project going. At first, we didn't know what we wanted to do; we just wanted to work on something together. We emailed and tossed out ideas. We started to realize that, while intersectionality has been a central concept in women, gender, and sexuality studies for decades, a full development of the application of the idea had not yet happened to our knowledge in theology. Intersectionality is the recognition of the simultaneity of multiple social identities within interlocking systems of oppression—people experience always and at once their gender, race, sexual identity, ability, age, social class, nation, and religion, and those intertwined identities locate them in relation to structures of power and domination.

While some liberation theologians have utilized the notion of intersectionality to frame, for example, queer black feminist theologies or postcolonial Asian feminist theologies, as far as we could tell, no one had articulated a method for theologians to use theories of intersectionality to construct fuller theologies that take into account both the theologian's own social location and the diverse and sometimes competing and conflicting theologies of people from other social locations. And so we decided this was a significant gap that we would attempt to address.

Grace lives in Pennsylvania and Susan in Oregon. So we were working through email, but we realized we needed to meet face-to-face to map out the structure of the book. Susan traveled to Pennsylvania, and, sitting in Grace's local Wegmans, we started to flesh out our idea. We realized, first and foremost, the book had to begin with a centering of the black feminists who named and developed intersectionality. Intersectionality's roots in black feminism cannot be overlooked or minimized. That intersectionality developed within black feminism is a crucial awareness in understanding the complexities and intricacies of the theory/method. While intersectionality's application has grown beyond black feminism, its roots in the experiences of black women must be acknowledged to situate the idea in its intellectual history.

As we talked more about intersectionality and making its application to theology, we realized that we needed to contextualize intersectional theology as a narrative, as well as a liberation, theology. We decided the best way to do this was to put our own stories side by side so readers could see the difference social differences within structures of power make, and how these different experiences and locations affect the ways Grace and Susan do theology. Like other liberation theologies, intersectional theology is contextual; it begins in the stories of those who are doing the theologizing, and it is always aware of the intersections of identities and the impact of structures of power. So, for example, as we explain in chapter 2, our locations led us to related but different conceptions of suffering—*han* for Grace and process theology for Susan—to analyze our experiences within patriarchal institutions of family and church. For both of us, intersectionality deepens and complicates our theologizing as it urges us to move from a focus solely on our subordinate identities in our theologizing to more complex understandings of self as simultaneously disadvantaged and privileged by virtue of our intersecting identities within systems of power and domination.

Next, we wanted to suggest ways theologians could apply intersectionality to their own theologizing. Drawing from the work of various feminist scholars and theologians, we adapted the questions of intersectional thinking to the process of theologizing specifically. As we developed these questions and asked them of theology ourselves, we discovered incredibly interesting, surprising, and disrupting possibilities. We thought of God as perhaps embodying multiplicity and contradiction rather than singularity and cohesion; we wondered how baptism could serve as both a marker of entry into a community and an invitation to engagement beyond the boundaries of Christian faith; we imagined what an intersectional church might look like and what its practices might be.

In fact, we realized that last question was so important that we devoted a full chapter to ecclesiology because we believe this is the place where intersectional theology may have the greatest applicability and impact. Intersectionality, as its theorists note, is biased toward justice. For the church, this means its understanding of its mission, its membership, its worship, and its activities should be shaped by their trajectory toward justice. Intersectional theology as a practical theology can provide critiques, challenges, and directions for the church as it seeks to be an inclusive, equitable, and just community of faith.

These are the concerns that framed the book for us. Our hope is that this introductory volume serves to introduce intersectionality and its possible applications to theology, to raise consciousness of the impact of social location and structures of power, to help readers see new paths in theology that might not be seen otherwise without an intersectional lens, and to encourage people of faith to work toward the community of love and justice envisioned by Jesus.

For most of Christian history, written theology has been the purview of educated, heterosexual, white, Western men. Challenges to the homogeneity of Christian theology arose in the mid-twentieth century through theologies of liberation that gave historical and social context to those doing the theologizing. Latin American, feminist, *minjung*, womanist, mujerista, and queer theologies emerged to contest the assumed neutrality and objectivity of white, male theologies. Recognizing the importance of social location for how theology is done and its contents, these theologies centered the marginalized and articulated theologies from below. While the center shifted to diverse identities, these theologies still tended to be mono-focused, or what feminist scholar Vivian May calls "gender-first" or "race-first," an approach that gives priority to one facet of identity as explanatory for experiences of oppression. And so, white feminists often wrote about gender as if it were a monolithic category, overlooking or minimizing the ways race and sexuality shape individuals' experiences of gender. Latin American liberationists wrote within a context of struggle in Central and South America but did not address the role of gender in the ethnic and class struggles of Latin America. In feminist theory, however, black feminist thought gave rise to the notion of intersectionality, rooted first in the work of Anna Julia Cooper and moving through the work of the Combahee River Collective, Audre Lorde, Patricia Hill Collins, and others. Intersectionality recognizes that people experience multiple and intersecting systems of oppression and domination simultaneously. Rather than applying "single-axis" thinking, intersectional analysis relies on "both/and," an analytical lens that allows for the complexities and contradictions of holding positions of dominance and subordination at the same time and having those concurrent locations mold and fashion experiences that are not race or gender or race plus gender but are rather the confluence of race and gender into something that is both and neither.

To a great extent, theologies, including many theologies of liberation, have not taken intersectionality into account. In particular, theologies written by heterosexual, white men rarely delve into the social location of the writer, exempting the writer's own whiteness, heterosexuality, and maleness from consideration in the theologizing he does. May is quick to remind us that an intersectional lens is not simply for members of subordinated groups. Everyone has race, gender, sexuality, ability, and so locations of dominance are as important in intersectional analysis as places of subordination. Until intersectional thinking is at the core of theology, theologians will continue to produce works that undertheorize the role of overlapping social differences in the development of theologies and will proceed as if theologizing can somehow be an objective and neutral process not centered in the person doing the theologizing.

Intersectionality recognizes how power works across multiple forms of difference and acknowledges that oppressive powers cannot be isolated or examined separately from one other. Rather, intersectionality pays attention to the ways social differences give shape to one another and demands that remedies to discrimination and oppression also attend to these intersections.

Theology as a social practice is not exempt from the effects of intersectionality. As a part of what feminist sociologist Patricia Hill Collins calls "the matrix of domination,"[1] that place where intersecting social identities and institutions of power overlap, theology plays a role in maintaining hierarchies of power. Christian theology specifically has been a key player in reproducing systems of oppression throughout history through its support for imperialism, capitalism, slavery, segregation, the domination of women, and anti-LGBTQ discrimination. In recent years, Christians have misused Scripture and theology to maintain social inequality, and, most recently, many Christians have supported the anti-woman, anti-immigrant, anti-people of color, anti-LGBTQ, and anti-poor rantings and policies of the present administration.

Intersectional thinking, then, is also a praxis. It is not simply a way of theorizing, but it is also a means for coalition-building to work toward social justice. Intersectional thinking can restore an activist center to our theology, demanding that what we think is not disconnected from what we do and asserting the priority of engagement with the world for positive social change for the most marginalized as the end goal of our theologizing. In this way, theology is never removed from the real lives of

---

1. Patricia Hill Collins, *Black Feminist Thought: Knowledge, Consciousness, and the Politics of Empowerment* (Boston: Unwin Hyman, 1990), 221–38.

human beings and their suffering; it is never something that ends with ideas, but always translates into action.

In this introductory book, we call for a prioritizing of intersectional thinking in the doing of all theology. The time has come for Christian theology to center intersectionality in its biblical interpretations, theologies, and church practices. We cannot develop feminist theologies without attending to race, sexual identity, social class, ability, gender identity, and age. We cannot develop queer theologies that do not account for race and class, for age and ability. We cannot develop racial/ethnic theologies that do not attend to gender and sexual identity. Heterosexual white men can no longer write theologies as if their own gender, race, and sexuality are not deeply embedded in the theologies they write. When we create a singular identity as normative for any liberatory theology, we marginalize the intersections of diverse people within a group, who experience oppressions in varying ways because of the intersections.

We propose an Intersectional Theology, a theology that begins in the intersections and moves toward liberation and justice for all people inclusive of all their differences. We propose an intersectional hermeneutic that begins with examinations of the biblical text's imperial history and highlights the intersectional lives of biblical characters—Jesus, a Jewish man of the working class living under a colonial power; Paul, a character full of challenges and contradictions as a Jewish man and Christian convert with Roman citizenship; the Samaritan woman; the hemorrhaging woman; the Canaanite women; the Ethiopian eunuch; Peter; and Cornelius. We propose an intersectional theology that leaves no one out, that leaves no one's experience unconsidered in exploring and expanding our ideas of God, sin, redemption, and the church, and that leaves no one's oppression unchallenged and no system of oppression intact.

A truly intersectional theology is messy. It encompasses all the contradictions, differences, and difficulties of human experience, and that means that sometimes we won't find a direct line from point A to point B to ultimate Truth. Instead, we will find questions, people who are nothing like us, ideas that terrify and challenge us.

An intersectional theology will not allow us to ignore human suffering, nor will it allow us to cause suffering in the name of God because it will underline the equal value of all of us toward our collective, contradictory, scary, and exhilarating understandings of God. This kind of intersectional thinking is for all of us, not just those of us who are members of an oppressed group. In fact, the embrace of intersectional thinking by dominant groups is absolutely essential to progress for us all because dominant groups hold the social, economic, political, and religious power to make significant change.

If we Christians begin to think this way, to center questions of the role of the intersections of difference in our theological thinking and faith practice, then we can revolutionize theology and the church, making them leaders in changing the world for good, rather than being followers twenty-five years behind the rest of society.

In our present political climate, we desperately need an intersectional theology to offer a prophetic call to the church to engage theologically and socially in resistance to the institutions and ideologies that perpetuate oppression. In centering intersectionality, we answer the call of the "least of these," and we position the church not as a complicit institution but as a leader in a vision toward God's kin-dom that welcomes, affirms, encourages, and supports all of God's children in all of their God-given complexity.

Intersectional theology, then, also calls for a deep listening. Heterosexual, white, Western, male theologians have not historically listened to the voices from the margins, particularly in such a way that those voices informed their own theologizing. White feminists have not always listened to the voices of women of color; liberation theologians have not always listened to women; black liberation theologians have not always listened to LGBTQ people—and these diverse people have also always existed in their midst. So, intersectional theology calls for listening both across and within differences. Intersectional theology invites us to listen beyond our comfort zone, to seek out the different, even the disrupting voices of those at the margins of social and religious power and to take seriously the challenges of their experiences and perspectives for theology. In this way, intersectional theology is an act of faith; it trusts we can find God speaking in our neighbors, our friends, and sometimes in people with whom we have little in common. It is a spiritual discipline that invites us to profound attentiveness to others, to ourselves, to the social and religious matrix that locates us in relation to power, and to the movements of God's spirit and the call to justice throughout it all.

OUTLINE OF THE BOOK

This book begins by introducing intersectionality. It defines intersectionality broadly and provides a history of the emergence of intersectionality as a central idea in feminist theorizing. Drawing on the work of Kimberlé Crenshaw and other black feminist thinkers such as Patricia Hill Collins, Audre Lorde, Vivian May, Ange-Marie Hancock, Johanna

Butler, bell hooks, and Beverly Guy-Sheftall, this chapter examines how intersectionality arose as black women examined how gender and race complicated one another in their own experiences and then follows the development of intersectional thinking as other women of color applied intersectionality to their own experiences as Asian American, Latina, Native American, or multiracial feminists and as queer and trans people expanded the concept to challenge heteronormativity and gender essentialism in feminist theorizing.

At the center of intersectional work is a commitment to examine how systems of oppression (sexism, racism, heterosexism, classism, ableism) shape and influence one another in the lived experiences of diverse people. Intersectional thinking demands attention to power and privilege as well as oppression and requires feminist thinkers to recognize their own privilege simultaneously with claiming space for their oppression. This chapter lays the groundwork for developing an intersectional theology by applying the scholarship of intersectionality to theological method.

Chapter 2 tackles "Biography as Intersectional Theology." This chapter draws on our own personal stories as examples for intersectional thinking. Grace's story centers on her experiences as an Asian American, immigrant, heterosexual minoritized woman in the Presbyterian tradition, while Susan's story centers on life as a white Southern lesbian who grew up in the Southern Baptist tradition before moving to the West Coast and becoming a member of the United Church of Christ. In their overlapping stories as women challenging sexist norms in society and the church, their accounts of their early church experiences, calls to ministry, theological education, marriages, ordination, and ministries make these intersections of gender with race, sexual identity, social class, and age visible and demonstrate the movement of biography as theology through an intersectional lens.

The third chapter examines how we do intersectional theology. This chapter offers an elaboration of intersectional theology and asks the question, "What happens when we move intersectional thinking to the center of theological analysis?" Intersectional theology shifts the nuances and complications of multifaceted identities and contexts from the margins to the center of theologizing. No longer can theologies emerge from a single source of identity as if that identity encompasses the whole of human experience. Instead, as a contextual theology, intersectional theology complicates other theologies of liberation by reminding that no single identity accounts for the complexities of human experience or theological understanding. Instead, theological thinkers must keep in mind the intersections of all forms of social difference and the systems of oppression that shape people's experience.

Intersectional readings of biblical texts expand and enhance the development of intersectional theology. The story of Ruth and Naomi is a helpful biblical story to draw on to imagine an intersectional hermeneutic. Ruth was of a different ethnicity than Naomi, but she engaged with her mother-in-law's people and became an important part of Jesus's history. They were both poor women who contested the interlocking power structures of wealth and patriarchy. An intersectional lens also helps us delve deeper into the stories of the Christian Testament where the struggles of women and men, Jews and gentiles and Christian converts are always inflected by the context of imperial power in which they live.

Intersectional thinking also helps us wrestle with some of Paul's challenges and contradictions as someone located in complex power relations as a Jewish man with Roman citizenship. As a critical lens for biblical interpretation, intersectionality helps us understand the dynamic of the social location of authors and actors in the biblical narrative—the Samaritan woman, the hemorrhaging woman, the Canaanite woman, the Ethiopian eunuch, Peter, and Cornelius—all of these stories take place within "the matrix of domination" that shapes the narrative around gender, race/ethnicity, sexuality, nation, and social class.

This chapter imagines intersectional theology as a method and offers initial applications of this method to key theological questions, such as the nature of God, sin, salvation, and the church. We make connections with other theologies of liberation and emphasize the ways intersectionality demands a theology that is contextual, destabilized, and tentative. Works produced by Delores Williams, Ada Maria Isasi-Diaz, Chung Hyun Kyung, Nancy J. Ramsey, Elizabeth A. Johnson, Elisabeth Schüssler Fiorenza, Kwok Pui-lan, Patrick Cheng, and others are important in developing a theology that uses intersectionality as a lens to tackle key doctrines of the church. Central to intersectional theology is movement toward justice through resistance to sexist, racist, heterosexist, classist, ableist, and ageist oppression and decentering of power, privilege, and dominance and through the building of a beloved community that encompasses the diversity of these intersections.

The fourth chapter focuses on intersectional theology as praxis. This chapter calls on readers to imagine what it would look like for individual Christians and the church as a whole to center intersectionality in their/its practices. As a liberatory practice, intersectional theology means Christians must relinquish their individual privilege and work toward the dismantling of systems of oppression. Christians can no longer ignore racism, sexism, heterosexism, classism, ableism, and ageism. We need to name these intersecting oppressions as sin and move toward reimagining a community that can live out this intersectional theology. This section explores possible applications of intersectional theology in the lives of individual Christians and the lives of faith communities and the church as a whole. In particular, we examine what an intersectional theology might mean for the church's internal functions—membership, baptism, communion—and also the church's work in the world, particularly in our current political climate that has targeted already-marginalized people, often in the name of God.

Intersectional theology is a new way of doing theology that takes seriously the interconnectedness and interrelatedness of power, hierarchy, and oppression. In understanding that oppression occurs on many interlocking personal and institutional levels, we must continue to challenge theology to engage in ongoing reimaginations of theology for a more just society. In light of our introduction to intersectional theology, this book aims to offer hope and shalom in a world full of uncertainty, inequitably distributed power, and subjugation, to move us toward God's kin-dom of peace, inclusion, equity, and justice.

1.

Introduction to Intersectionality

While law professor Kimberlé Crenshaw coined the word "intersectionality" in 1989,[1] the notions of overlapping and converging identities and social institutions had been part of black feminist thought since the days of Anna Julia Cooper and Ida B. Wells. Crenshaw gave a name to this concept that explains how black women's experiences of the ways overlapping identities (in this case gender and race) uniquely shape their experiences as "black women" within social institutions, such as work and law. Crenshaw drew specifically from court cases that highlighted the ignored effects of intersections in the lives of black women. In *DeGraffenreid v. General Motors*, for example, five black women sued General Motors for discrimination. They claimed that General Motors' system of seniority disadvantaged black women because the company had not hired black women prior to 1964 and that made black women most vulnerable to the seniority-based layoffs that cost all of the black women hired after 1970 their jobs during a recession. The court found in favor of General Motors, declaring that black women were not a special class to be protected. The court stated that the lawsuit either had to claim discrimination on the basis of sex or on the basis of race but not both. General Motors, the court pointed out, had hired women long before 1964—white women—and therefore the plaintiffs could not claim sex discrimination. The court also dismissed the race discrimination claim and encouraged the plaintiffs to join another race-discrimination complaint against GM. The women refused, noting that their claim was one

---

1. Kimberlé Crenshaw, "Demarginalizing the Intersection of Race and Sex: A Black Feminist Critique of Antidiscrimination Doctrine, Feminist Theory and Antiracist Politics," *University of Chicago Legal Forum* 1 (1989): 139–67.

of both race and sex discrimination. The court reiterated its belief that "black women" were not a protected category, affirming what Crenshaw explains as protections that only apply if black women's experiences coincide either with the experiences of white women or of black men.[2]

In naming intersectionality, Crenshaw gave social justice theorists and activists an important tool for analyzing the nuances and complexities of oppression. The word has now become ubiquitous in social justice theory and practice, but its roots in the theorizing of black women are crucial to a full understanding of its multifaceted and simultaneous analysis and application, particularly as we move toward developing a method of intersectional theology.

WHAT IS INTERSECTIONALITY?

Intersectionality is a tool for analysis that takes into account the simultaneously experienced multiple social locations, identities, and institutions that shape individual and collective experience within hierarchically structured systems of power and privilege. In other words, intersectionality is a lens for understanding how gender, race, social class, sexual identity, and other forms of difference work concurrently to shape people and social institutions within multiple relationships of power. It is kaleidoscopic, constantly rendering shifting patterns of power visible. It is confluent, a juncture point where identities, locations, institutions, and power flow together creating something new. It is a praxis—an ongoing loop of action-reflection-action—that integrates social justice–oriented theory with activism toward social justice on the ground so that theory informs practice and practice informs theory.

Social justice is a structuring of institutions and relationships so that people's basic needs are met, people are treated with equity and fairness, differences are welcomed and valued, and economic, social, political, and religious equality is achieved. Intersectionality's greatest impacts have been in community organizing toward social justice and in the academy in fields such as women, gender, and sexuality studies, ethnic studies, and cultural studies and, to some extent, in more traditional disciplines such as sociology, law, and political science. For example, theories of intersectionality have been central in the transformation of women, gender, and sexuality studies as a discipline so that issues of race/ethnicity, sexual identity, social class, ability, and other forms of difference are deeply and inextricably embedded in contemporary feminist thought

---

2. Crenshaw, "Demarginalizing the Intersection," 141–43.

and pedagogy. In STEM fields, intersectional thinking has led to examination of the disparate experiences of white women, women of color, and LGBTQ scientists and engineers in the field and recent analysis of the impact of social differences on the way science itself is done and interpreted. Intersectional analysis helps us understand why Latina and black women scientists are frequently mistaken for janitors, when their white counterparts are not,[3] or why the gender and sexual identity of a scientist or research subject can affect the results of a study.[4] Using an intersectional lens helps us view phenomena in more complicated and nuanced ways that pay special attention to social differences, institutions, and power.

The next sections provide a brief overview of the history and workings of intersectionality that can begin to advance theological thinking toward an intersectional center.[5] Traditionally, theology has assumed a white, male, heterosexual, able-bodied subject with very little self-reflection on the impact of theologians' social location on theology. In other words, for most of Christian history, straight white male theologians have spoken for everyone else, as if their theologies do not reflect the bias of their own social positions and power. This has meant that our theologies have been partial, a reflection of only a very small slice of the whole of human experience. In many ways, we have missed out on a great deal we could have learned about God and ourselves by ignoring and subordinating the experiences and theological reflections of most of humanity. An intersectional center demands that theology attend to difference and power and recognize the significant contributions to theology from diverse contributors and the limitations of theologies that only reflect a dominant or single-axis view.

---

3. Brigid Schulte, "Black and Latina Women Scientists Sometimes Mistaken for Janitors," *Washington Post*, February 6, 2015, https://tinyurl.com/ycxdrqrq.

4. Richard Harris, "A Scientist's Gender Can Skew Research Results," NPR, January 10, 2018, https://tinyurl.com/ybbbulns.

5. For a full explication of the complexities and nuances of intersectionality, however, we suggest Vivian M. May's *Pursuing Intersectionality, Unsettling Dominant Imaginaries* (2015), Ange-Marie Hancock's *Intersectionality: An Intellectual History* (2016), and Patricia Hill Collins and Sirma Bilge's *Intersectionality* (2016). These works offer much greater depth than we can provide in this introductory volume and will serve as significant sources of information, questions, and challenges for those seeking to do intersectional theology.

A BRIEF HISTORY OF INTERSECTIONALITY IN BLACK FEMINIST THOUGHT

Women's and gender studies professor Vivian May defines intersectionality as "a justice-oriented approach to be taken up for social analysis and critique, for political strategizing and organizing, for generating new ideas, and for excavating suppressed ones, all with an eye toward disrupting dominance and challenging systematic inequality."[6] This complex understanding of intersectionality as a theory and an action-oriented method has evolved in the past few decades across the diversity of feminist scholars, but its roots are firmly in a tradition of black feminist thought that gender studies and political science professor Ange-Marie Hancock roots in black women's activism.[7]

As early as 1851, Sojourner Truth raised issues of intersections of race and gender in her famous "Ain't I a Woman" speech in which she highlighted the interplay of race and gender in contemporary designations of womanhood. Anna Julia Cooper's 1892 *A Voice from the South by a Black Woman of the South* anticipated intersectionality, recognizing the links between her race and her gender. Also, in the 1890s, Ida B. Wells connected issues of race and gender in her anti-lynching work.

Feminist activist Frances Beal's 1969 essay, "Double Jeopardy: To Be Black and Female," critiqued sexism within the Black Power movement and racism within white feminism. The 1977 Combahee River Collective's statement added heterosexism to the mix of interlocking systems of oppression. The Collective noted that they found it "difficult to separate race from class from sex oppression because in [their] lives they are most often experienced simultaneously."[8]

Poet and womanist scholar Audre Lorde identified the American "mythical norm" as "white, thin, male, young, heterosexual, Christian, and financially secure" and warned that people could not simply identify only the way(s) they are outside the mythical norm but they must also acknowledge the ways they also benefit from the facets of identity that reside within the mythical norm.[9] For example, she noted the ways white women often assumed gender as the "primary cause of all oppres-

---

6. Vivian M. May, *Pursuing Intersectionality, Unsettling Dominant Imaginaries* (New York: Routledge, 2015), 228.

7. Ange-Marie Hancock, *Intersectionality: An Intellectual History* (New York: Oxford University Press, 2016), 38.

8. Audre Lorde, "A Black Feminist Statement," in *Words of Fire: An Anthology of African-American Feminist Thought*, ed. Beverly Guy-Sheftall (New York: The New Press, 1995), 234.

9. Audre Lorde, "Age, Race, Class, and Sex: Women Redefining Difference," in *Sister Outsider: Essays and Speeches*, 2nd ed. (Berkeley, CA: Crossing Press, 2007), 116.

sion" while ignoring differences of race, class, sexuality, and age among women. Moreover, she argued that oppressed peoples cannot give priority to one form of oppression over another but must engage all of the intersections at the same time:

> I was born Black, and a woman. I am trying to become the strongest person I can become to live the life I have been given and to help effect change toward a livable future for this earth and for my children. As a black, lesbian, feminist, socialist, poet, mother of two including one boy and a member of an interracial couple, I usually find myself part of some group in which the majority defines me as deviant, difficult, inferior, or just plain "wrong."
>
> From my membership in all of these groups I have learned that oppression and the intolerance of difference come in all shapes and sexes and colors and sexualities; and that among those of us who share the goals of liberation and a workable future for our children, there can be no hierarchies of oppression. I have learned that sexism and heterosexism both arise from the same source as racism....
>
> Within the lesbian community I am Black, and within the Black community I am a lesbian. Any attack against Black people is a lesbian and gay issue, because I and thousands of other Black women are part of the lesbian community. Any attack against lesbians and gays is a Black issue, because thousands of lesbians and gay men are Black. There is no hierarchy of oppression.
>
> I cannot afford the luxury of fighting one form of oppression only. I cannot afford to believe that freedom from intolerance is the right of only one particular group. And I cannot afford to choose between the fronts upon which I must battle these forces of discrimination.[10]

For Lorde, the struggle against oppression must, of necessity, be multifaceted and simultaneous because oppressions by sex cannot be separated from oppressions by race, by class, by sexuality, by age. By giving voice to the need to attend to our simultaneous locations of oppression and privilege and declaring her refusal to parse out one identity over another, Lorde articulated key facets of intersectional theory that underline the complexities of identity that must be central in intersectional thinking.

In 1990, sociologist Patricia Hill Collins further complicated our understandings of how power is organized by elaborating the "matrix of domination," the means by which intersecting oppressions are regulated through social institutions such as the family, government, education,

---

10. Audre Lorde, "There Is No Hierarchy of Oppressions," in *I Am Your Sister: Collected and Unpublished Writings of Audre Lorde*, ed. Johnetta B. Cole and Beverly Guy-Sheftall (New York: Oxford University Press, 2009), 219–20.

and religion.¹¹ Her concept recognized the importance of context for analyzing how the matrix of domination organizes oppression. While oppressions of gender, race, class, and sexuality are all embedded in the matrix, the ways relationships of power are structured around these differences vary from context to context. She explains, "Domination is structured differently" in different times and places. In other words, "The universality of intersecting oppressions" is "organized through diverse local realities."¹² Collins adds social institutions as another significant variable that must be considered in examining systems of oppression. So, for example, in a chapter on the black church, anthropologist, women's and black studies scholar, and former college president Johnetta B. Cole and women's studies professor Beverly Guy-Sheftall note, "The Black church is an institution that is a critical site for the subordination of women and the perpetuation of conservative gender ideologies on the one hand; and a place where womanist and feminist theologians challenge such ideas and practices of inequality and envision the kind of 'beloved community' that is constructed on principles of gender equality."¹³ Womanism is an anti-sexist, anti-racist, anti-imperialist theoretical lens that centers the experiences and perspectives of black women.

Other black feminist thinkers such as Beverly Smith, Angela Davis, Cheryl Clarke, bell hooks, and Barbara Smith have added to the complex understandings of how difference and power work at the intersections. And while intersectionality is clearly rooted in the work of black women, other women of color have also engaged in furthering complex and nuanced thinking in their own political struggles. Cherrie Moraga and Gloria Anzaldúa's coedited collection of writings by radical women of color, *This Bridge Called My Back*, was an important early work in drawing together the distinct yet overlapping experiences of gender, race, class, and sexuality in the theoretical, autobiographical, poetic, and artistic works of women of color. Anzaldúa also developed the concept of *mestiza* consciousness that derives from living in the "borderlands," her image for the in-between spaces occupied by those who embody multiple oppressed identities. Other important works that highlight distinct, overlapping experiences arose from Asian American women such as Cathy Song and Kitty Tsui (*Making Waves*¹⁴) and Native women

---

11. Patricia Hill Collins, *Black Feminist Thought: Knowledge, Consciousness, and the Politics of Empowerment*, 2nd ed. (New York: Routledge, 2000), 227–28.

12. Collins, *Black Feminist Thought*, 228.

13. Johnetta B. Cole and Beverly Guy-Sheftall, *Gender Talk: The Struggle for Women's Equality in African American Communities* (New York: Ballantine, 2003), 105.

14. Asian Women United of California, *Making Waves: An Anthology of Writings by and about Asian American Women* (Boston: Beacon, 1991).

such as Elizabeth Martinez (*Unsettling Ourselves*[15]). While a great deal of intersectional thinking centers on the Global North, women of the Global South such as Musa Dube and Kwok Pui-lan have also raised issues of transnationalism and cross-border relationships. Each of these approaches highlights the particular struggles faced by women based on different races, sexualities, classes, and ages and underlines the need for building alliances and coalitions across differences.

UNDERSTANDING INTERSECTIONALITY

Intersectionality, Vivian May explains, is a "problem-solving approach."[16] It is action-oriented, and so perhaps the better question is not what *is* intersectionality, but what does it *do*?[17] As a liberation politics, intersectionality makes power visible,[18] particularly where resistance and dominance often collude to subordinate nuances and complexities of intersections.[19] Importantly, intersectionality is not an additive approach;[20] rather it is an approach that holds multifaceted identities and systems of oppression in mind as simultaneous and mutually shaping forces that situate people differently within the matrix of domination. This complex and nuanced thinking moves us away from single-axis analysis (gender or race or sexuality) to matrix thinking, allowing us to attend to in-group inequities as well as inequities across groups.[21] It rejects either/or thinking in favor of both/and, and it demands real-world applications to everyday life and to social structures.[22] As Patricia Hill Collins and Sirma Bilge remind us, intersectionality's focus on people's real lives opens space for diverse perspectives;[23] in other words, different people provide different analyses of the same phenomena. And in intersectional thinking, this analysis is always biased toward justice.[24] As Vivian May explains, intersectionality is not neutral: "Intersectional work takes a stand against inequality and harm and overtly aims for social transformation and meaningful change."[25]

15. Unsettling Minnesota Collective, *Unsettling Ourselves: Reflections and Resources for Deconstructing Colonial Mentality*, 2009, https://tinyurl.com/ycqtzgxu.
16. May, *Pursuing Intersectionality*, 19.
17. Patricia Hill Collins and Sirma Bilge, *Intersectionality* (Cambridge: Polity Press, 2016), 5.
18. Hancock, *Intersectionality: An Intellectual History*, 57.
19. May, *Pursuing Intersectionality*, viii.
20. May, *Pursuing Intersectionality*, 3.
21. May, *Pursuing Intersectionality*, 4.
22. May, *Pursuing Intersectionality*, 5.
23. Collins and Bilge, *Intersectionality*, 18.
24. May, *Pursuing Intersectionality*, 28.
25. May, *Pursuing Intersectionality*, 28–29.

Keeping intersectional thinking at the center, however, is not easy. May warns of "slippages" that can send us back into single-axis thinking.[26] For example, in an attempt to make intersectionality more "universal," we may actually depoliticize or deracialize it.[27] In other words, we can argue that everyone's identity is intersectional without exploring the political ramifications of those differences within systems of hierarchical gendered and racialized power. Intersections are not just about identities; they are also about institutions and systems of power that also intersect and give shape. We can also create hierarchies of oppression that slip from intersectionality's core commitment to simultaneous multifaceted analysis. bell hooks illustrates this when she contends that feminists should not try to bond over shared experiences of victimization as women or some abstract notion of womanhood, but rather they should bond over a shared political commitment to ending sexist oppression.[28] We also lose sight of the intersections when we focus on the oppressions that affect us without paying attention to the ways systems of power and privilege also advantage us at the same time. As early as 1983, feminist scholar and publisher Barbara Smith noted the difficulty, for example, for many liberation groups to include heterosexism in their analysis. She wrote, "Despite the logic and clarity of Third World women's analysis of the simultaneity of oppression, people of all races, progressive ones included, seem peculiarly reluctant to grasp these basic truths, especially when it comes to incorporating active resistance to homophobia into their everyday lives."[29] May cautions that such single-axis thinking universalizes the experiences of some as if they can represent all, obscuring differences within groups, as well as the power relations that work in and between groups.[30] Ange-Marie Hancock worries also about the possibilities of the co-optation of intersectionality when scholars attempt to use it within the existing ontological and epistemological frameworks of their disciplines. It thus becomes a "tool for reform at the margins" rather than a "framework with the potential to radically reform our structures of government and public policies, as well as to make other changes."[31]

For Collins and Bilge, key to intersectional analysis is understanding how power is organized. They note four "distinctive yet interconnected

---

26. May, *Pursuing Intersectionality*, 15.

27. May, *Pursuing Intersectionality*, ix.

28. bell hooks, *Feminist Theory from Margin to Center*, 2nd ed. (Cambridge, MA: South End Press, 2000), 47.

29. Barbara Smith, "Homophobia: Why Bring It Up?" in *The Truth That Never Hurts: Writings on Race, Gender, and Freedom* (New Brunswick, NJ: Rutgers University Press, 1998), 112.

30. Smith, "Homophobia: Why Bring It Up?," 82.

31. Hancock, *Intersectionality: An Intellectual History*, 13.

domains of power: interpersonal, disciplinary, cultural, and structural."[32] The interpersonal domain of power is the domain where individuals interact and relate to one another across various advantages and disadvantages. The disciplinary domain of power is how the rules work, how power operates to "discipline" people's lives through the options afforded or not afforded to them. The cultural domain of power is the ideas and messages that shape our understandings of difference and power (the playing field is level; we live in a meritocracy where people are rewarded according to their effort). Finally, the structural domain of power is the mutually reinforcing relations of gender, race, class, sexuality, nation, and social institutions.[33] Through these four domains, power and resources are distributed inequitably across differences, producing and reproducing social inequality.

CORE CONCEPTS OF INTERSECTIONALITY

Collins and Bilge delineate six core concepts of intersectionality that will be especially useful in developing an intersectional theology:[34]

1. Social inequality: Intersectionality recognizes the simultaneous and multiple factors that contribute to social inequality. Rather than seeing social inequality as the product of only one factor—class or gender or race—intersectionality challenges us to see social inequality as the product of the interactions of difference within social institutions.

2. Power: Power is constructed, maintained, and distributed in the interactions of gender, race, nation, and other forms of difference within interlocking systems of oppression. Power relations, Collins argues, must then be analyzed both at the intersections and across the domains of structural, disciplinary, cultural, and interpersonal power.[35]

3. Relationality: Relationality demands a both/and approach rather than an either/or approach. It centers interconnections and complicated relationships rather than single factors or static entities.[36]

---

32. Collins and Bilge, *Intersectionality*, 7.
33. Collins and Bilge, *Intersectionality*, 7–13.
34. Collins and Bilge, *Intersectionality*, 25–30.
35. Collins and Bilge, *Intersectionality*, 27.
36. Collins and Bilge, *Intersectionality*, 28.

4. Social context: All power relations occur within a context, and so intersectional thinking requires we consider the historical, social, intellectual, political, and religious contexts that give shape to our analysis. This approach opens up the possibility for distinct and differing perspectives that add to and complicate our own and helps us understand difference itself.[37]

5. Complexity: By refusing a single-axis analysis, intersectionality creates space for complexity, fluidity, and even contradiction in our understandings of power, privilege, inequality, and resistance. This complexity is what makes intersectional thinking so difficult and inclines us toward "slippages" if we do not keep intersectionality at the forefront of our thinking.

6. Social justice: Intersectionality, as May has argued, is biased toward social justice. We engage in intersectional thinking in order to act in the world to bring about change that dismantles oppressive systems and creates inclusive and equitable systems for all people.

Intersectional analysis, then, functions with its bias toward justice to uncover and restructure power relations by dismantling oppressive ideologies, practices, and institutions. Activist and scholar Angela Davis demonstrates the importance of intersectional thinking in her analysis of the women's movement. She challenges white feminists who acted as if progress for women were a separate issue from race and social class, as if there were "such a phenomenon as abstract womanhood abstractly suffering sexism and fighting back in an abstract historical context." She points out that such an abstraction can only arise when analysis of gender occurs in isolation from intersections with race and class: "That state of abstraction turns out to be a very specific set of conditions: white middle-class women suffering and responding to the sexist attitudes and conduct of white middle-class men and calling for equality with particular men. This approach leaves the existing socioeconomic system with its fundamental reliance on racism and class bias unchallenged."[38]

To avoid these slippages, May encourages us, then, to understand intersectionality as an epistemological practice, an ontological project, a coalitional political orientation, and a resistant imaginary.[39] These concepts will prove essential in developing intersectional theologies.

As an epistemological practice, intersectionality "attends to knowers'

---

37. Collins and Bilge, *Intersectionality*, 28.
38. Angela Davis, *Women, Culture, Politics* (New York: Vintage, 1989), 18.
39. May, *Pursuing Intersectionality*, 34.

social location."[40] It includes lived experience and rejects any assumption of a normative center.[41] Because intersectional thinking assumes all knowers are situationally located in different relations to power, it underscores the inherent political nature of knowledge and the production of knowledge. Knowledge, then, is not objective and neutral but deeply embedded in power relations, and so intersectionality calls for questioning of who is an authoritative knower, who has access to knowledge, who has access to the production of knowledge, whom does knowledge serve?[42] Because those with greater social power have typically had greater access to the production and distribution of knowledge, their ideas have usually prevailed as dissenting narratives have been silenced and made invisible. Intersectional thinking uncovers these hidden discourses and affords them epistemological privilege in understanding how power and oppression operate.

As an ontological practice, intersectionality highlights multiplicities of identities. In other words, people are "ontologically plural"; they exist simultaneously in multiple relations to power and identities; they are at the same time constrained by power, resistant to hierarchy, and often complicit with domination.[43] This means intersectionality understands identities not as separable entities but as thoroughly integrated, mutually shaping and reinforcing forces. Identity categories, however, are not static essences but shifting frames in and through which people experience the world. They are not, as sociologist and women's studies professor Irene Gedalof explains, "straightforward descriptions of pre-existing realities but are discursive constructs that continually produce the realities they claim to describe."[44] Insisting that we are "the same and different," rather than privileging one identity over another, emphasizes how identities are constituted by intersections so we understand that gender is not separable from race or sexual identity or other factors.[45] Intersectional thinking allows us to understand people as more than a single aspect of identity. Instead this both/and approach allows for the complexities and contradictions and refuses fragmentation of the self into the atomized compartments of either/or thinking. May argues that rather than fixed positions, identities are orientations toward the world that

---

40. May, *Pursuing Intersectionality*, 34.
41. May, *Pursuing Intersectionality*, 34.
42. May, *Pursuing Intersectionality*, 34–36.
43. May, *Pursuing Intersectionality*, 39.
44. Irene Gedalof, "Sameness and Difference in Government Equality Talk," *Ethnic and Racial Studies* 36 (2012): 3.
45. May, *Pursuing Intersectionality*, 42.

allow us to plumb intersections, overlaps, contradictions, complicities, and resistances.[46]

Significantly, intersectionality is also a coalitional politics; it challenges us to work together across differences to create change toward social justice in such a way that we do not fragment ourselves or deny any aspect of ourselves. American studies professor Duchess Harris calls it "polyvocal."[47] A coalitional politics toward social justice requires a self-reflexivity that pays attention to our privileges as well as our oppressions and recognizes that we may have to give up some of those privileges in order to engage in the work of justice.

Finally, May argues, intersectionality is a resistant imaginary. Intersectionality calls for us to shift the center, to move the experiences of the marginalized from the periphery and to hear the voices of those who are usually silenced by social power and hierarchy. This re-membering of otherwise neglected histories can help us see the disjunctures and disruptions of multiplicity and can make hidden resistances visible.[48] In other words, intersectionality demands a "countermemory" that reads the existing archive "against the grain."[49] This lens helps us see the history and effects of imbalanced power relations and denaturalizes oppression by uncovering its operations. It allows us to question the historical accounts we have been given and explore the silences to unearth the stories of those marginalized within dominant discourses. Intersectionality then creates space to create the stories to which we should have had access,[50] and so to a great degree intersectional thinking relies on the re-membered imaginations of poets and novelists as well as sociologists and theologians.

WHY DOING THEOLOGY AT THE INTERSECTIONS MATTERS

Intersectionality is significant for theology in a number of ways. For too long, theology has been done by white heterosexual Western men who have treated theology as something pure, pristine, and nonsyncretistic. Theology has mostly been a monochromatic and one-sided discourse that does not take seriously voices from the Global South or

---

46. May, *Pursuing Intersectionality*, 47.
47. Duchess Harris, "'All of Who I Am in the Same Place': The Combahee River Collective," *Womanist Theory and Research* 2 (1999): 16.
48. May, *Pursuing Intersectionality*, 53.
49. May, *Pursuing Intersectionality*, 54.
50. May, *Pursuing Intersectionality*, 59.

voices of women or voices of other marginalized groups. This singular one-sided voice has dominated much of our Christian history to the detriment of groups of people it marginalized. Therefore a new method and approach to doing theology is long overdue and necessary. Engaging in a new theology that will be liberative for all people and especially for the oppressed and the marginalized is critical.

New forms of liberation theology emerged in the 1960s that took seriously the context and social location of those who were experiencing oppression, subordination, and marginalization. But these liberative voices were mostly one-dimensional in tackling and understanding their marginalization and oppression. In search for a theology that examines and takes seriously the interconnectedness of lives and the intersections of oppressive powers, we believe that intersectionality is an essential tool in developing a liberative theology for the oppressed and marginalized across and inclusive of all differences.

Intersectionality as a method for theology can be significant and meaningful. Vivian May explains, "Everyone has intersecting identities and all of us live within interlocking structures of raced and gendered social stratification."[51] In other words, each of us has gender, race, sexual identity, social class, and other forms of social difference, and we all live within relationships and social institutions that confer advantage and disadvantage based on those identities. As May argues, intersectionality is "relevant to and *'about' all of us*, and *it is not neutral*."[52] This matters for theology because we do theology from those identities and within those interlocking systems of oppression. Certainly the contextualized theologies of liberation take note of the identities and systems that shape the theologians engaged in feminist, queer, womanist, Latin American, and other forms of liberation theologies. Many times, however, even these contextualized theologies neglect a full account of the ways identities and institutions overlap and shape one another. They may shift the center to an oppressed group, but they often remain single-axis forms of theology. For example, Latin American liberation theology focused primarily on socioeconomic disparities between rich and the poor. As a new way of doing theology, Latin American liberation theology arose out of poor base communities that experienced poverty and lack of economic resources for their families and community. Yet this new focus did not consider the impact of other junctures with economic oppression. Despite its commitment to reforming the economic landscape for the poor, Latin American liberation theology failed to examine issues

---

51. May, *Pursuing Intersectionality*, 25.
52. May, *Pursuing Intersectionality*, 12.

of colonialism, gender, race, and sexuality that interconnect and overlap with socioeconomic concerns.

On the other hand, a great deal of traditional/systematic theology proceeds as if matters of context, social location, and systems of oppression are irrelevant to the doing of theology. Vivian May's point, that all people have intersecting identities, is particularly salient when applied to traditional/systematic theology because white, heterosexual men do still write from a particular social location that is often rendered invisible and assumed to be normative. In other words, traditional/systematic theology proceeds as if it is somehow neutral and objective, built only from sacred texts and/or reason, somehow divorced from the overlapping identities and social location of its authors.

For example, one of the most influential theological voices of the twentieth century was Karl Barth, who relied on the Bible and did not value context or social location when doing theology. Barth's work appeared in response to much of the liberal theology that offered an enculturated understanding of theology. Barth wanted to disassociate any human search for or approach to God, as Barth believed in a top-down theology. For example, Barth understood the Spirit as coming from above and not from below. For Barth, revelation in Jesus Christ was not only sufficient: it was also complete.[53] According to Barth, we come to know God through Scripture and thus do not need categories such as the social sciences, psychology, science, and literature to help us do theology. Revelation is complete in Jesus.

Ange-Marie Hancock's explication of intersectionality also reminds us that intersectionality is not a concept that can simply be added to the theological toolbox. Instead, intersectionality should radically reform the ontologies and epistemologies of theology so that issues of social difference, power, and justice are always central in our theologizing. Drawing on literary and social theory traditions, she argues that we produce knowledge within interpretive communities and these interpretive communities have particular gendered and racialized histories that matter in the knowledge they construct.[54] For theology, this means that the whiteness, maleness, and heterosexuality of most theologians throughout history matters and should be subject to interrogation as much as their reasoning and biblical exegesis. Going forward, this means that the theologies of the future should no longer proceed as if social locations and systems of oppression are irrelevant; rather theologies, including those written by white, heterosexual men, must shift epistemologies to begin,

---

53. Kirsteen Kim, *The Holy Spirit in the World: A Global Conversation* (Maryknoll, NY: Orbis, 2007), 33, 34.

54. Hancock, *Intersectionality: An Intellectual History*, 16.

not in abstraction or in a text, but in a context that shapes abstract reasoning and textual analysis. And that reasoning and analysis should, as May argues, be biased toward justice.

DOING THEOLOGY AT THE INTERSECTIONS

Vivian May offers four commitments that theologians can borrow to guide theologizing that is intersectional:[55]

1. "Honor and foster intersectionality's antisubordination orientation." Because it is biased toward justice, intersectionality rejects the subordination of individuals or groups. For theology, this suggests focused attention toward constructing theologies that purposefully destabilize structures of power and facilitate inclusion and equity.

2. "Draw on intersectionality's matrix approach to meaningfully engage with heterogeneity, enmeshment, and divergence." May encourages us to keep on center differences within categories so we don't negate in-group differences and ignore the impact of, for example, the intersection of race with gender. This also allow us, she argues, to unearth "layers of suppressed meaning" and "unpack" dominant explanations. In theology, this attentiveness allows us to ask unexpected and disruptive questions and problematize assumed and accepted conventions.

3. "Take up intersectionality's invitation to follow opacities and to read against the grain." Reading against the grain invites us to approach traditional theological notions with skepticism and to make visible the workings of power in our usual way of thinking about theological doctrines and practices. It encourages us to move the voices of the marginalized to the center of our theologizing and recognize theological sources outside the typical norms of traditional theologies.

4. "Set aside norm emulation as a philosophical/political/research/policy [and we would add '/theological'] strategy." Intersectionality invites theology to challenge its own disciplinary norms and to embrace imaginative, challenging, and disruptive ways of doing theology that resist hierarchy and work toward justice. An intersectional approach demands that we rethink

55. May, *Pursuing Intersectionality*, 229.

our ways of doing theology and formulate theological methods that embed an intersectional lens.

Embracing intersectional thinking means that we should approach doing theology by questioning assumptions that are rooted in the norms of dominant culture, purposefully pursuing justice, embracing the complexities and contradictions, and refusing to do theology as usual. A recent example of such intersectional work in theology is womanist queer theologian Pamela R. Lightsey's *Our Lives Matter: A Womanist Queer Theology*. Lightsey ties her intersectional theologizing closely to the aims of justice. She writes, "Not unique to womanist scholarship is this work's intersectional analysis that explores the impact of race, gender, class, gender identity, and sexual orientation on the theological understandings of LBTQ Black women. These points of departure from what some call 'orthodox' Western theology remain critical to the work of womanist scholars because these subjects are significant to the peace and reconciliation of the peoples of this global world."[56] Significantly, she also identifies her orientation and history in the Wesleyan tradition of the United Methodist church as another axis of identity to be analyzed as part of her intersectional work.

While some thinkers critique contextual and intersectional thinking as breaking people apart into smaller and smaller units, intersectional thinking does not lose its broader relevance to all of us by its attention to the specific details of individual lives. Instead, intersectional thinking adds complexity to our theologies that is more reflective of the diverse realities of differently situated lives. The ever-changing subjects of intersectional thinking challenge theologies that declare themselves absolute truth and remind us that none of us has a decontextualized and unmediated knowledge of ultimate reality or the divine. To approach an approximation of larger realities we must be inclusive in our analysis to account for diversity, and we must be directed toward justice as we center our examinations of power and hierarchy as inherent parts of our theologies.

We imagine intersectional theology as kaleidoscopic. Intersectional theology is a destabilizing theology that reminds us that our theological ideas are always tentative, and theology is always an ongoing process. A kaleidoscopic theology is one that is constantly changing with each turn of perspective; it holds multiple (and sometimes competing) views in mind at the same time. It makes visible the differently situated knowers and the complex web of relationships and social institutions in which

---

56. Pamela R. Lightsey, *Our Lives Matter: A Womanist Queer Theology* (Eugene, OR: Pickwick, 2015), xx.

it is embedded. It is contingent and recognizes its own rootedness in the social location of the theologian and within interlocking systems of oppression. Significantly, it is also self-reflexive, always interrogating itself for possible complicities with structures of subordinating power and seeking relevancy toward social justice for all people.

Intersectional thinking is rooted in and values narrative ways of knowing.[57] It is always contextualized and pays attention to differently situated knowers. For intersectional theology, this means story is a starting place, particularly subjugated stories that illuminate the mechanisms of power across identity categories and social institutions within systems of oppression. In the next chapter, we offer a comparative and contrasting telling of some of our own stories to reveal the workings of difference and power in our own lives and to demonstrate the movement from story to theology that is intersectional.

---

57. May, *Pursuing Intersectionality*, 20.

QUESTIONS

1. What is your social location? Where do your gender, race/ethnicity, sexual identity, social class, ability, age, nation of origin, and religion intersect and situate you within structures of social, political, economic, and religious power? How does your social location affect the ways you do theology? How can this awareness help you be attentive to the theologies of people who are differently located and allow those theologies to be in dialogue with your own beliefs?

2. Why is situating our understandings of intersectionality within black feminist thought essential for work toward social justice?

3. What assumptions undergird your theology? What assumptions might people in other social locations hold? How might those assumptions challenge or enhance your own?

4. How has your theology been formulated in an either/or framework? Does a theology of both/and seem inviting to you?

5. How has a single-axis thinking limited your perspective or understanding of your own experiences? How has single-axis thinking universalized your experiences as if they represent all people's experiences?

6. We produce knowledge, including theology, within interpretive communities. What role does your interpretive community play in how you think about God, sin, salvation, the church? How might other interpretive communities add to your understandings?

7. This chapter touched on power and power relations. Have you experienced power negatively? How can power be used for building each other up and working toward justice?

8. How do you ensure your theologizing is not complicit with structures of domination and subordination? How do you ensure your theologizing is biased toward justice?

2.

Biography as Intersectional Theology

Intersectional work is deeply personal. Each of us has multiple intersecting identities formed in our interactions with other people, social institutions, and systems of oppression. These intersections and interactions give shape to individual identities that are different from and more than the individual facets of gender, race, sexual identity, social class, ability, age, nation, and religion that constitute the self. More importantly, these intersecting identities situate us differently within hierarchies of power; in other words, we are advantaged and constrained simultaneously within interlocking systems of oppression depending on the intersections of our various identities. No one identity, then, is fully explanatory for any facet of the self or any experience of advantage or disadvantage.

Intersectional theology invites us to think about our individual stories as "both/and." Rather than seeing ourselves as victims or oppressors, intersectional thinking demands we recognize the simultaneity of our location as persons with both dominant and subordinate identities that give unique shape to our experiences, both across groups and within groups. The value of narrative as intersectional theology is that it opens the space for us to see, examine, and value the complexities, intricacies, contradictions, and individuality of each person's experiences in a way that more linear and systematic theologies do not. Rather than subordinating distinctions or outliers in favor of majority or dominant group expressions, intersectional theology makes room for the specific, the idiosyncratic, the overlooked and marginalized that may be speaking in God's still, small voice. By attending to differences and commonalities across all stories, intersectional theology disrupts the dominance of the theologies of the mythical norm and makes visible the operations of power at the center of traditional theologies. It also invites the suppressed knowledges and theologies of the dispossessed into the heart of the theological enterprise, even as it demands recognition of the intersections of dominant identities among oppressed groups. In other words, the theologies that arise from intersectional thinking remind us that we all are situated simultaneously both as privileged and disadvantaged, and these locations matter in our experiences and in the ways we do theology. Intersectional theology can enhance systematic theology through its humbling reminder that the theologian's social location matters, even in the best attempts to arrive at a comprehensive and internally logical and consistent theology. Intersectional theology also reminds us that we cannot really do theology for others; rather we do theology alongside others. We accept with humility the limitations of our theologies from our own social locations, and we embrace theologies arising from sometimes complementing, sometimes competing narratives of people different from ourselves.

For example, we (Grace and Susan) never do theology simply as women. In fact, we do not do theology simply as a Korean American woman and a white American woman. We do theology as an educated, financially stable, middle-aged, able-bodied, heterosexual, Christian, immigrant, Korean American woman and an educated, financially stable, middle-aged, able-bodied, lesbian, Christian, native-born American, white woman. As we explore our stories below, we see how these differences and similarities matter and how they shape the theological perspectives we each add to Christian discourse. We both have experienced sexism, but our experiences of sexism have been mediated by the other facets of our identities in such a way that our experiences of sexism, while similar at times, are actually different. We also recognize that many of these identities are much less stable than others—we won't be middle-aged forever. We weren't always from the educated middle class. We also recognize that these are only our stories and cannot represent any of the groups of which we are a part, although they do add to our collective understandings of theology. We offer our stories here to see in a side-by-side comparison and contrast how intersectionality works and to imagine how an intersectional theology can emerge from our highly personal and particularized stories and yet still speak to larger questions about God, humanity, redemption, and other theological themes. More importantly, as Vivian May has pointed out, our stories can highlight intersectionality's bias toward justice and guide our theologizing toward God's just kin-dom.

INTERSECTIONALITY AND OUR IDENTITIES

Our theological ideas do not exist separately from the stories of which they are a part. Stories give rise to convictions and provide contexts for exploration of theological ideas. Our stories interact with the metanarrative of Christian faith and the attendant theologies that have been handed down to us, but our stories also become places where we test the ongoing validity of these ideas and recognize their contributions and their limitations as we test them in different historical times and social locations. In this way, our stories form a kind of theology in themselves that is in dialogue with systematic theologies. This back-and-forth reminds us that theologies are at best partial and tentative; they are always contextualized and local; and they often need to be transformed in light of new experiences and perspectives that emerge in God's ongoing revelation. Our stories are part of this process, this give-and-take of theology, and we offer them, not as representative, but as particular and individual and thus able to add to our collective knowledge about God. Intersectional theology recognizes that we need all the stories. Because each of us is uniquely located in relation to difference, power, hierarchy, and privilege, we each have some piece to add to the whole fabric of theology; we each offer something others need to learn, and we each need to learn what all others offer.

GROWING UP: GRACE

As I look back, all my work, teaching and writing, has been about intersectionality and, more specifically, intersectional theology. In my work, I did not always refer to my life experiences, but my life experiences informed all my work, with the intersections at the center.

I was only five years old when I immigrated with my parents and sister from Korea to Canada in January 1975. Korea had gone through a terrible war and the country was torn apart. Economically, Korea was not stable, and it was important to my dad to leave and begin a new life in a different country with new possibilities. We landed in Toronto and stayed there for a few weeks before moving on to London, Ontario, about two and a half hours west of Toronto. Growing up in London was not easy for an immigrant family. In the 1970s, London, Ontario was a mostly white city of about 250,000 people. We lived there from 1975 to 1985.

When our family immigrated we didn't have much money. And as a child, I always understood that we never had enough money. My older sister and I rarely did extracurricular events that required money, as I never could bring myself to ask for money from my struggling parents. We barely had enough to survive and were just getting by.

I attended a predominantly white public school, Glen Cairn, with children from mostly lower-income to lower-middle-class families. I walked to school every day, passing all the small family homes and wishing that I lived in one of those homes rather than our tiny, bug-infested two-bedroom apartment. We didn't have much furniture and what we had was secondhand furniture that my dad picked up from the garbage or from someone who was going to throw it away. Our old burgundy living room couch squeaked every time you sat on it or got up. The springs were popping up on the left side, so you always had to be a little careful when you sat on that side. My mother tried to make it more desirable by putting an ugly forest-green sheet over it. She said that the couch was "dirty," so she had to make it clean to sit on. One day I overheard my parents talking, and my dad said he found the couch near the dumpster and asked some people to help him bring it home for us to use.

Economics played a big role in forming my identity. I wanted so many things growing up, but my parents could not afford them. The only doll I ever had was a hand-me-down doll that my dad picked up somewhere. It was a tiny doll with blond hair, blue eyes, and a pink flowered dress. I played with it all the time. Since my parents never had extra money, I was in a situation of never having enough—clothes, books, toys, or things other kids had.

We had a bit of money in Korea that my grandmother gave to my dad to invest. But as soon as we immigrated, we lost much of that money due to bad investments with acquaintances. We struggled with basic day-to-day needs. We rarely ate out, and the only real forms of entertainment were our small black-and-white television or the games we played outside. I only remember seeing a movie in a theater twice during my childhood. But it wasn't just the socioeconomic status that was hard for me as a child; it was also the cruel racism that I experienced in my public school.

I remember being taunted on the school playground almost daily. Many kids used slang insults such as *ching chong, ching chong* toward me. They made fun of my eyes and not just mine but those of the children of the other five or so Korean immigrant families who attended the school. White kids pulled their eyes sideways or slanted and mocked us by saying they had Chinese and Japanese eyes.

They objectified me and asked, "What are you?" They did not ask me *who* I was, but *what* I was. I am not sure why they wasted their energy asking me that daily, but they did. It was a living nightmare to be part of this "game" that the school kids played with me.

The taunting at school was painful for me, as I was a vulnerable child and not emotionally strong. I became ashamed of my own cultural heritage and wished I were white like the rest of the kids at school. Growing up in-between two cultures meant that I straddled the white and the Asian culture. I was trying my best to fit in both but feeling that I didn't fit in either of them. I was trying to fit in the Asian community so that I could please my parents and honor them. I spoke in "broken" Korean to them; I attended a Korean church and a Korean-language school. My parents wanted me to learn as much about Korean history, language, and culture as I could, so I immersed in it as much as possible. But as I did all this, I felt like a misfit at school. My English was poor, and I wasn't accepted into the dominant white culture and felt like a cultural misfit. I tried my best to fit in but couldn't. I straddled two cultures and didn't fit in either of them.

Asian culture puts a lot of emphasis on honor and shame. In such a culture, it was shameful to experience racism within my life. It was even shameful to talk about it or share it with my own parents. Since I did not discuss my feelings of shame with them, I do not know if they ever knew the shame I experienced. Finding an outlet for my shame and for all the pain of racism was difficult.

I had a tough childhood trying to figure out my own identity and trying to find out why people made fun of me. Mine was a childhood filled with turmoil, shame, and anxiety that lasted into my teens. I had difficulty understanding myself and who I was. I wondered how life would be if I were white. Some of my Korean friends dyed their hair. They also put clear sticky tape on their eyelids to make a "double" eyelid so that their eyes would look bigger and less "Asian." Some of my Korean friends refused to speak Korean at school anymore because the other kids made fun of them. It was tremendously difficult to just be who I was and be happy with my Asian culture and heritage.

The mocking wasn't any worse for me than it was for my Korean male friends. We were both equally made fun of due to our ethnicity, different looks, and different culture. Our economic status could have contributed to the mocking. Since my parents didn't have much money, we just wore hand-me-downs from friends and family. Some of the hand-me-downs were from another decade and were noticeably unfashionable by the time I started wearing them. I grew up in the 70s, and the clothes were from the 60s. The pants I wore were too long or too short; the shirts were baggy or tight. I wore them because I had no other options. My parents didn't have the financial means to buy new clothes for us.

Being a girl in an Asian immigrant household was complex for me. As a girl, I had to fulfill all the womanly work of cooking and cleaning the house. In a Korean immigrant household, whether you worked just as many hours outside the home as a man didn't matter; you still had to cook and clean whenever you came home. It was double-duty for many Korean women. They were expected to carry out the duties of being a wife, a mother, and a daughter-in-law. It was a tough life for many women.

My mother's life was no exception. Because my father didn't earn enough money at his job as a factory worker, going from one job to another to support us, my mother also worked in a garment factory. She had the pain of trying to appease my dad and trying to rest after a long day's work. My mother left for work before we kids left for school, but, before she left, she put our cooked breakfast on the kitchen table. She also made our lunches and left them in the oven for us to eat when we came home every day for lunch during elementary school. She came home after we did, and as soon as she arrived she began cooking dinner. After we ate, she cleaned up and prepared for the next day's meals. If my dad didn't want to eat the meal my mom made, he forced her to cook him something else. Some nights she spent a lot of time in the kitchen.

My mom hardly complained. She knew that complaint would translate to anger from my dad. At times, it felt like everything that was done inside the home was to make sure that my dad was happy.

My father secretly wished for a boy. In the Asian patriarchal culture, a son carried on the family name and legacy while a daughter was thought to belong to her husband's family. It became almost necessary for people to have a son to carry on the family lineage. My parents had two girls: my older sister and me, and this probably saddened my father. The status of my gender had a negative impact on my childhood, especially in my family and my Korean Presbyterian church.

At home, my dad expected to be waited on hand and foot. He never cooked, did the dishes, or cleaned the home. He made it known that it was the women's job to do that. My mother worked just as much as my dad or even more, but she was always expected to cook and clean whenever she got home from work. After school, we came home and ate snacks as she prepared dinner for us. It felt like she was always busy doing something for us, while my dad got to rest, read, and live more comfortably. Watching my mother suffer like that at home was difficult.

It felt like my dad lived as a king, while my mother, my sister, and I were his servants.

This type of sexism was also experienced in the church. It was clear that the men had all the power and were the head of the church. They were the ministers, elders, and leaders in the church. They made all the decisions and they "told" the women what to do. When I was growing up, I never saw any women preachers in the church. Sexism was woven into the ways that I was taught to read and interpret the Bible. I never knew that women could even be preachers, as the only preachers that came to my church or any of the churches that I visited were men.

Women in the church were marginalized just as they were in the home. In both, they were responsible for food, housework, and children. As a patriarchal institution, the church used the name of God to block women from ascending to leadership and ministerial roles, roles that had power. The male leaders believed this structure was theologically correct and what God had commanded. Furthermore, all the language used in the church about God was masculine. Every prayer started with "Father God," and there was no concept of feminine imagery of God. Only men were created in the image of God, and therefore women were subordinate and needed to be obedient to men.

Growing up in such a strict patriarchal household was hard. The women had to obey the men, since God had ordained men to be the head of the house. It was difficult for me to wrap my head around this, and what it meant for our family. We needed to be able to share and talk with each other, but it was difficult to know how to handle the racism and sexism that we faced.

GROWING UP: SUSAN

Rome, Georgia had desegregated a few years before I was born in 1960, and so, although I never saw "Whites Only" signs, I was still born into the white supremacy of Southern racism. My family was working class—my father was a welder and pipefitter at a paper mill; my mother was mostly a stay-at-home mom, although she began to work first as an assistant to a justice of the peace and then as a substitute elementary schoolteacher after my sister and I had both started school. My father had a union job that meant higher wages and good benefits, and so, while we did not have a lot of money for name brands and extravagances, we always had enough for a house my parents bought, enough for food, clothes, cars, and a few vacation days on the beach. Neither of my parents had attended college, but they put a premium on education, and I always knew that a college education was in my future. I also knew I'd have to earn an academic scholarship to afford to go to college. Despite our working-class status, we considered ourselves middle class. We certainly knew in the racial hierarchies of the 1960s in Georgia that, while we were not rich, we were still better off than any of the black folks in town.

That I was a girl was a disappointment to my father. My maternal grandmother told me he had wanted a boy. That I was not a girly-girl was a disappointment to my mother, who dressed me in frilly dresses and encouraged me to play with dolls. Early on I chafed at the expectations of white Southern womanhood. I did not enjoy wearing dresses or playing with dolls. I wanted to play football. I have a photo of my family from 1964. It's Christmastime, and we're visiting my father's sister's family. Two of her children were boys, just a couple of years older than I was. My mother sits off to the side, wearing a maternity dress. My sister would be born that next June. I'm dressed in a red velvet dress with a lace collar and black patent-leather shoes. I'm also wearing my cousin's new football helmet, and I'm down in three-point stance with my father. I had just turned four a few days earlier.

I also knew very early in life that I wanted to do ministry. My parents were devout Southern Baptists, and so a local Baptist church was the first place I went, at the age of six weeks, and I was immediately listed on the cradle roll. I loved church for as long as I can remember. I felt welcomed and valued there. At the time, I didn't notice that part of the reason I felt so welcome was probably that most of the people in the church were pretty much like me—white, working and middle class, and fundamentalist. Still, that Southern Baptist church planted the seeds of discontent.

While the church excluded women from being pastors or deacons or even Sunday school teachers of men, it also told me I could be anything God called me to be. This is the message I heard, even as "women libbers" advocated for women's rights and Helen Reddy sang "I Am Woman." I resonated with the women's movement, and I resented the ways the church treated the boys differently from the girls. While we made gift bags for missionaries, the boys played basketball. While we had to wear dresses, the boys wore jeans. I knew something was not right.

The contradictions didn't stop there. We sang about how Jesus loved the little children, red and yellow, black and white, but we also avoided driving through the parts of town where black people lived, and we were nervous when the first few black people came to our church. By the time I was in high school, the conflict between these two competing perspectives was too great. I remember quite clearly telling the last racist joke I would ever tell. While it was still hanging in the air, I was struck by a firm conviction that racism was wrong, and I knew I'd never tell another racist joke again. That conversion soon led me to anti-racist commitments that continued to grow throughout my seminary experience.

Of course, unpacking my white privilege would become a lifelong commitment. Growing up, I never realized that my comfort with the church's metaphors—my sinful soul was black but could be made white as snow—stemmed from my own racial privilege. Even as I packaged toothbrushes and toothpaste for missionaries, I did not need to question the church's role in the colonizing efforts that subordinated Africa and the Americas. And even though by high school I was able to name my own racist attitudes and acts as my individual sins, I did not yet understand the collective sin of racism in which my entire privileged life as a white girl was embedded. Those understandings would only come in adulthood as I began to hear and take seriously the voices of people of color from the US, Latin America, Africa, and Asia.

CALLING: SUSAN

When I was twelve years old, I walked the aisle during an altar call and took the pastor's hand to tell him I had been called to ministry. Of course, at the time the pastor, the congregation, and even I thought this meant being a missionary or a religious educator. The pastor and congregation may have added pastor's wife to that list, but that never crossed my mind. I was already ambitious enough, competitive enough, and strong-willed enough to know that, whatever that calling, it was mine—my career, my ministry, and not adjunct to someone else's.

After college, in January 1982, I enrolled in the Southern Baptist Theological Seminary in Louisville, Kentucky. These were the early days of the controversy among Southern Baptists, which was purportedly about biblical inerrancy and theological fidelity, but, as I have argued elsewhere,[1] was really about women. And so my identity as a woman in ministry was forged in conflict as the same Southern Baptists who had sent me to seminary tried to erect barriers for women—we were not to be pastors; we were not to be ordained; we were to submit graciously to our husbands. While I didn't go to seminary with a calling to the pastorate, many of my peers did, and, as I heard them preach and saw them minister, I recognized in a new way the deeply structured sexism of the Southern Baptist Convention. Undoubtedly, God had called these

1. *God Speaks to Us, Too: Southern Baptist Women on Church, Home, and Society* (Lexington: University of Kentucky Press, 2008).

women, and, truth be told, they were as a group much more talented than many of the men at seminary who faced no barriers of gender when they professed a calling to ordained ministry.

I became an avowed feminist my first semester in seminary. While I would not have considered myself particularly radical at the moment, my trajectory had changed. Slowly I came to realize that I did not want to work at a denominational agency editing curriculum materials. I wanted to be a professor . . . of religion.

My first tenure-track job was at a small Southern Baptist college in California. The state's pastors and parents weren't particularly ready for a young (twenty-six-year-old) feminist teaching religion. At least once every couple of weeks, the college's president or dean pulled me aside to tell me that someone had called to complain about me. Sometimes the complaints were about the documentary hypothesis. Many times they were about my refusal to relegate women to second-class citizenship in the church, family, or society. While I was in seminary, I saw in the controversy at the national level how harmful and hateful Christians could be. At the Baptist college, I experienced it firsthand. I saw clearly the operations of power and the ways theologies were deployed to concentrate power in the hands of conservative white men acting in concert to quell the advances of women. And I realized with a devastating clarity that the collusion of individuals with structural inequities and systematic sinfulness was crushing and that sometimes righteousness did not prevail.

I fled to Oregon and an evangelical Quaker college. I had not sought ordination while at the Baptist college. That surely would have gotten me fired. At the Quaker school, I realized that the eight Quaker men in the religion department were all "recorded," an official acknowledgment of gifts of ministry, and I, the lone woman, had no official sanctioning. I did not like the message that sent to my students.

I still attended a Southern Baptist church, but I knew they could not ordain me because they would have been kicked out of the state convention. Instead, I asked the church I attended in seminary to ordain me, and so in 1993 I returned to Louisville to be ordained. In Southern Baptist life, ordination is a local church issue, and so, despite the Convention's opposition to women's ordination, local churches continued to ordain women, and I was among the first 500 women ordained in Southern Baptist life.

During seminary, I had come to the conviction that the segregated worship hour in Christian churches was a sinful legacy of racism, and so I committed to becoming part of churches that honored and embodied anti-racism. In Louisville, I found Shalom Baptist Church, a small, biracial inner-city congregation with racial reconciliation at its core. This is the church that ordained me. Years later, after I left Southern Baptists when the Convention amended its constitution to exclude congregations that supported LGBT people, I found a home in a United Church of Christ congregation that is intentionally multiracial, multicultural, and open and affirming.

CALLING: GRACE

I grew up in a Korean Presbyterian church in London, Ontario. It was a conservative church where men held all the leadership positions and women were relegated to the kitchen. There are various types of Presbyterian churches and the one that I attended as a child was conservative and different from the Presbyterian Church in Canada (PCC), which is the church I later belonged to in my late teens. It was really difficult for me to watch women be told to "be silent" in the church and commanded to listen and obey men, who are the "head of the household." I struggled with this patriarchy that was so embedded in the church and especially the Korean church. There were clear, distinct gender roles in the church. The women were relegated to the kitchen and were not allowed to preach or have any leadership roles within the church. I was encouraged to fulfill my female gender roles by acting passively, wearing dresses, remaining silent, and obeying the men in the church.

When I finished tenth grade, my parents moved to Toronto and started to attend another Korean Presbyterian Church. At the new church, I had a wonderful youth pastor who encouraged me to explore, question, and reread Scripture from a liberative perspective. All the gender roles that felt constraining were suddenly lifted as he encouraged me to read Scripture contextually and introduced me to biblical hermeneutics.

When I was seventeen, I felt a call to serve God. The call process was a struggle, as I never grew up with female church role models who were ministers or elders. With no female role models, I was not sure how I was going to do God's work in a male-dominated church and ministry. I kept my calling to myself and my youth pastor, who then encouraged me to get an MDiv degree. I was not too sure how I was going to serve God, but I studied theology after my undergraduate degree in psychology. I entered the program not sure if I wanted to do ministry in a church or teach theology after I graduated.

The Presbyterian Church in Canada was already ordaining women, so I didn't face any ordination problems and became a candidate for ordination. The Presbyterian Church will ordain a candidate who pursues full-time or at least half-time ministry. Even though I was ready to be ordained, I decided to pursue my doctoral work instead and put my ordination on hold, as I couldn't study full-time and also engage in half-time ministry.

I started my PhD program in theology in 1995 at the University of Toronto and graduated in 2001. Most of my classmates were men at that time. Only a handful of women were in the program. One of the difficulties of studying with men were the Korean male students who kept giving me hints that I should be home having babies rather than studying. After graduation, I searched for a teaching position and also had my third baby in 2003. In 2004, I took a full-time position at Moravian Seminary. I felt a big difference in my experience of racism in the United States versus Canada. In the United States, much of the discussion on racism is grounded in the slavery of African Americans. But the discussion of racism in Canada involved all people of color. Therefore, it was difficult for me to talk about my experiences of racism in the United States and have people believe that it was actually racism.

When I moved to the United States, I restarted my ordination process. The ordination process for the Presbyterian Church (USA) requires four written exams, "preaching for a call," and being "under care" by a presbytery for a few years. I began the process again in 2008 and finally got ordained in 2011.

The ordination was a long and difficult process. When all the presbytery requirements for ordination were completed and the ordination date was chosen, the minister of the Korean Presbyterian Church suddenly became resistant to my ordination. He kept delaying my ordination date and giving me a hard time about my ordination. The date was set, but the minister gave the excuse that it needed to be postponed. My guess is that he found it hard to see me get ordained and thus wanted to push it back. This occurred several times before the final ordination date was set. Two weeks before ordination, he told me that he had the power to stop my ordination. He had no authority to do that, as it was the presbytery that was ordaining me, but he kept insisting that my ordination was up to him.

The Korean male pastor wanted me to obey and be subservient to him. This was very troubling and disturbing. After such a long, difficult process of getting ready for ordination, it was horrible to have a middle-aged Korean male pastor tell me that he had the power to stop my ordination. Even on the day of my ordination, he turned to me and asked me, "Do we have to go through with this?"

My ordination has opened doors for me to preach in many local and national churches. I feel called to preach, and I welcome the invitations to preach in many churches. However, I feel that my ordination within my local Korean church was not very welcomed. I am not often invited to preach at Korean churches, which says a lot about how Koreans may view my ordination status. Many Korean churches still don't believe in women's leadership in the church, and some still do not welcome women's ordination.

LOVE AND MARRIAGE: GRACE

When I was in my second year of seminary, a Korean pastor took me and two other Korean seminary students for lunch. At the restaurant, the Korean pastor proceeded to tell me that I was "over the hill." I was only twenty-four at the time, but he told me that in Korean culture, a woman should get married by twenty-three. He said that a twenty-one-year-old woman was considered silver, at twenty-two she was gold, and at twenty-three she was diamond. Thus twenty-three was the prime age for a woman to get married.

It was stressful to grow up in a patriarchal Asian culture that expects a woman to get married and have children. When a woman is not married by a certain age, people begin to think that there is something wrong with her and think that she is going to be an old maid—something undesirable and to be avoided at all costs. Thus the pressure continues for young women to hurry up and get married to a man. There is an assumption of heteronormativity within the Asian American culture. That same pastor also told me that God would be happier if I got married than if I studied. There was so much pressure to drop my studies and get married like a "good Asian woman." The Asian church was living out its faith in a dominant patriarchal culture where the purpose of a woman is to get married and give birth to a child to carry on the family lineage.

I ended up getting married to a Korean American man the summer I graduated from seminary and before I began my PhD studies. It was a happy moment for me. I felt the pressure from the Korean American society to get married lift and I felt that I could now begin to live my life and just move on.

We met at the Korean church that I was serving and got married after dating for over a year. It was a big wedding; lots of my parents' friends came, as it is common for Korean immigrants to invite their church to a wedding. My parents decided to invite their church and also their school alumni friends. Our guest list mushroomed to more than six hundred people.

But soon after marriage, I was under a lot of pressure to do daughter-in-law "duties," which added pressure on me and took time away from my own PhD studies. I was expected to host parties for my in-laws and do proper duties as a daughter-in-law. I was to be obedient to the in-law family and do as I was told. Growing up in Canada, I didn't expect this, but somehow I quickly got caught between two cultural marriage expectations. This became an added source of unexpected stress. On the other hand, my husband was finishing up his PhD studies and was very supportive of my own doctoral studies.

It was clear that women were subordinate to men in a marriage relationship, or so my in-laws told me. This reinforced the patriarchal biblical notions of women's subordination and their obedience to men. This was not just a biblical notion but also a very Asian patriarchal belief and teaching. To survive and have some sanity while trying to be a PhD student in feminist theology was a challenge.

Furthermore, there was added pressure from the male Korean dominant society to become a mother and not a student in theology. When I was beginning my comprehensive exams, I learned I was pregnant with my first baby. It was unplanned and a very stressful time. I was sick most of my pregnancy and felt that I would never finish my degree with a baby. But somehow I persevered and made it through my comprehensive exams and the writing of my thesis. I was actually eight months pregnant with my second child when I defended my dissertation.

The Asian patriarchal culture celebrated my pregnancy and wished upon me that I would give birth and become a "good" mother and stay home and quit my PhD studies. A male classmate actually told me that "God will be happier if [I had] a baby rather than have ten PhD degrees." He encouraged me to have more babies and be a good stay-at-home mother just like his wife. Biblical stories of wives taking care of their children were told to me repeatedly, as if being a mother and studying was the worst and most evil thing to do in this world. Many biblical stories like Sarah raising Isaac, and Mary giving birth and raising Jesus, were among the narratives that were told and retold to me.

LOVE AND MARRIAGE: SUSAN

Nothing in the worldview I was given made room for the possibility that I was gay. I understood myself as straight into my early thirties. In seminary, we had explored the biblical and theological understandings of sexuality that had led me to embrace a positive view of diverse sexualities, but I had not at the time thought of myself as anything but straight. Even as I had my first romantic relationships with women, I still thought, "I'm straight. I just happen to love her." Only in my early thirties did I finally acknowledge that there was a pattern. I kept falling in love with women. At that time, I became involved with my first out and proud partner who helped me also become out and proud. But it wasn't an easy journey.

I was still teaching at Christian colleges as I began my coming-out process. I struggled, not with feeling something was wrong with me, but feeling I was being unethical by remaining at institutions that were avowedly anti-gay. I feared being found out and fired. Even as I looked for a way to leave, I came to think of myself as a double agent—or a subversive living in occupied territory.

At last, the pressure became too great, and I walked out of teaching. I left an associate professor position with nothing lined up and no income beyond the summer. I spent a year in social services and feared I would never again hold a teaching job. Then a part-time instructor position opened at Oregon State University. I had completed a master's degree in women studies and English at OSU while I was still teaching at the Quaker college, and, while I was still in the closet at the Quaker school, I committed to myself to be out from the moment I set foot on OSU's campus. When I took the position there, I found a place where I could be whole and wholly myself.

A number of years later, I met the love of my life. The state of Oregon had been fighting anti-gay ballot measures for years, but OSU offered partner benefits and treated Catherine and me as any other couple. Of course, we still couldn't get married. It was 2007. In 2008, the state began to register domestic partnerships. Catherine and I were the fourth couple to register in Benton County the first morning that partnerships were available. She says we got "domesticated." One of the perks of "domestication" was that we could file our taxes jointly in the state, even though the federal government still did not recognize our relationship. To do the Oregon taxes, our accountant also had to fill out a federal form "as if" we were filing jointly for federal taxes as well. That "as if" form showed the difference if we could have filed together versus the federal requirement at the time that we file separately as single individuals. The difference was $10,000 more that we were required to pay in federal taxes than we would have if we had been a married heterosexual couple.

That summer after our January "domestication," we held a commitment ceremony. We still called it a wedding, even though it had no legal status. Our pastor officiated, 160 of our friends and family members came, we pledged our love and faithfulness, we ate cake and danced, but at the end of the night, in the eyes of the federal government and most of the states in this country, we still were not married. And so we spent thousands of dollars having legal papers drawn up to ensure power of attorney, healthcare power of attorney, inheritance, and other rights that married heterosexual couples automatically receive (and we were able to do this as a result of our class privilege since we were able to afford the lawyer's fees, unlike less financially stable gay and lesbian couples). We made sure to take these papers with us when we traveled out of state in case we ever needed to make decisions for each other. Slowly a number of states legalized marriage equality, although it still was not recognized by the federal government. We wanted to wait and get legally married in Oregon, but in 2013 the IRS declared it would recognize marriages performed in any state, and so we decided to go to Washington, just across the river in Vancouver, to get legally married. Oregon was on track to approve marriage in 2014, but the tax implications were so great we decided not to wait another year and lose yet another $10,000 in federal taxes. I referred to our Washington wedding (also performed by our pastor) as our "tax equity ceremony." Still, I cried, full of emotion, as I pledged my love and faithfulness again.

In June 2015 the US Supreme Court at last affirmed marriage equality. We wept with joy. And we listened in horror as pastors railed against people like us and this decision that recognized our love and humanity. We watched county clerks put their bigoted convictions above the law, and we despaired with every couple turned away, every hateful word spoken in the name of God. We still travel with our papers. Twenty-eight states continue to allow discrimination against LGBT people in employment and housing, and twenty-nine allow discrimination in public accommodation (such as restaurants and hotels). Even our papers don't protect us from that.

Ongoing discrimination against LGBT people in the United States is rooted in religious bigotry. In the name of terrible biblical exegesis, Christian people continue to exercise institutional domination over LGBT people. Sodom's sin was not homosexuality; it was inhospitality. And many Christians repeat this sin against LGBT people every day.

The intersections of race, class, nation, and region do afford Catherine and me more protections than many of our LGBT siblings. Particularly, because we live in Oregon—and in the progressive Willamette Valley, specifically—we are able to be out and sheltered from some of the threats faced by LGBT people of color or working-class LGBT people. Because I work at a university that values diversity, I no longer have to fear losing my job over my sexual identity. Because Catherine and I are both native-born Americans, we don't have to worry about having a partner deported or denied entry into the country. Still, when we leave the relative safety of the cities, we are wary, even in Oregon. The bigotry fueled by conservative Christianity toward LGBT people enables ongoing violence, and, since the election of Donald Trump, bias incidents against LGBT people (as well as people of color, women, immigrants, Muslims, and Jews) have increased.

Queer theologies have in recent years helped us destigmatize sexual difference and move sexualities to the center of our thinking about God. As intersectional theologies, they have also paid attention to the ways gender, race, and social class impact experiences of homophobia, particularly within the Christian church. Coming to terms with the centrality of human sexuality is a paramount task for theology, and intersectional thinking offers a way to help the church move beyond the harm it has done and continues to do by reinforcing gender norms and normative heterosexuality.

HAN: GRACE

It feels like I have been fighting racism or sexism throughout my life. These systems of injustice are embedded in our society and culture to marginalize, subordinate, and oppress people of color and women. This results in individual and communal suffering.

In Korea, there is a word that tries to capture the unjust suffering that occurs because of unjust systems set up to cause grave suffering. This Korean word is *han*. I was introduced to this word *han* from a young age. It is a common word, and I heard many elderly women use it constantly in their speech. My own mother use to talk about *han* whenever she experienced deep pain. Thus *han* was a word I was exposed to frequently and from a very young age.

As is often the case, foreign words are difficult to translate into other languages. One possible way to translate *han* is "unjust suffering" or "deep piercing of the heart" due to unjust systems. Injustices such as racism, sexism, homophobia, and so on all work to discriminate and oppress. As they do so, they cause deep pain and suffering to the oppressed. The pain is like a "piercing of the heart" that digs deep and causes trauma. Since systems are set up to create such pain, it then becomes necessary to work toward eliminating such pain, or *han*.

All individuals and communities suffer to a certain degree and for many reasons. People may suffer on a hot day because they don't have shade or air-conditioning. People suffer because they have to skip a meal because they forgot their lunch or are too busy to eat that day. This is not *han*. *Han* is the experience of unjust suffering because of systems that exist to cause suffering. When we examine Korea's colonial history, Japan had colonialized Korea from 1910 to 1945. Koreans experienced *han* as a people as colonialism robbed them of their culture, religion, and identity. This caused tremendous *han*, as Koreans suffered as a people. *Minjung* theology is a theology of the people and arose during the struggle for democracy in Korea after the Korean War. *Minjung* are the politically oppressed and economically exploited, and *minjung* theology tries to address the marginalized, the broken, and those who have suffered *han*.

In our present North American context, racism is entrenched in our culture and continues to discriminate, oppress, and subordinate people of color. Our society and religion are patriarchal, and this permits rape, sexual abuse, and oppression of women to continue. These forms of oppression give rise to *han* as people of color and women continue to suffer under unjust systems that keep them subordinated and dominated.

In theology, we want to work toward liberating ourselves from the damages of *han*. We want to eliminate *han*, which burdens our lives and creates unrest and tension in our lives. An intersectional theology works toward eliminating *han* in our lives. It does this by understanding that these unjust systems that cause *han* are interrelated and interconnected. Therefore, we cannot just address one issue but must address all these issues to move toward a just society without *han*.

PROCESS THEOLOGY: SUSAN

My greatest struggle of faith emerged from suffering—my own and others'. My fundamentalist pastors and Sunday school teachers had taught me that God controlled everything. They embraced Job's story unthinkingly. Somehow they did not find God's wager or Job's suffering problematic because, in the end, Job was faithful, and God restored him. They never talked about the dead children who didn't come back to life. My own suffering awakened me to the inadequacy of an all-powerful God. I realized that if God had had the power to stop my childhood sexual abuse and did not, then I could not, would not, love such a God. I could not reconcile what I knew of a God of love with a God who would allow a child to suffer in such a way. The answers my fundamentalist church had provided seemed trite and empty. My struggles at the Baptist college at the hands of people who professed to be doing God's work intensified my conviction of the insufficiency of the notion of an all-powerful, controlling God. Without an alternative to this idea, I was at the point of renouncing my Christianity.

Toward the end of my brief tenure in California, I became a visiting scholar at the School of Theology at Claremont and took a seminar on the philosophy of Alfred North Whitehead with John B. Cobb. Whitehead's philosophy informed Cobb's development of process theology, and process theology rescued me. In process theology, God is not coercive power but persuasive love. All suffering is evil, and, while God does not control the circumstances that create suffering, God suffers with the one who suffers and rejoices with the one who rejoices. God calls all things to fulfill their divine aim, and the goal of existence is enjoyment—being fully present and engaged in purposefully living the divine aim. Suffering, which can be caused by natural forces or human behavior, disrupts enjoyment and is therefore in opposition to the divine aim. While God does not control the forces of nature that cause suffering—hurricanes happen in nature, volcanoes erupt, people develop cancer—God does call each human to act in love and be at every moment the best human being that person can be. This is persuasive love. For me, this meant that God did not cause or allow my suffering. Human beings made choices that brought about my suffering. They sinned. God could not have intervened as a great deus ex machina and rescue me, but, through it all, God, as persuasive love, did call them to be better than they were. They did not listen. The most important realization for me, however, was that God suffered with me. I was never alone in my suffering. God's persuasive love was with me also, calling me to be something better, something more. By letting go of what I now understood as patriarchal notions of power embodied in particular ways in a notion of an all-powerful God controlling the universe, I embraced an immanent God whose love calls us to love and who opens a future that does not have to be determined by power over, hierarchy, and control but can be characterized by love, welcome, multiplicity, and connection.

CONCLUSION

Theology begins with experience. One cannot separate theology from one's experience, as the two are interconnected and inform each other. White European male theology has denied this, as if theology happens in a vacuum. But one cannot deny the presence of experience in their theology as is evident in Augustine's theological discussions on sin and grace that came from his own personal life struggles and Luther's understanding of justification by faith that arose from his experiences of being unable to confess all of his sins because there was always "one sin left unconfessed." Experience played a key role in how these early influential theologies were written and how they were understood.

Therefore, we must recognize the importance of experience in how we understand God in our world. People's experiences of imperialism and colonialism led to the rise of postcolonial theology. The experiences of poverty and socioeconomic discrepancy in Latin America led to the rise of Latin American liberation theology. Experiences of racism and discrimination led to the rise of black theology, Asian American theology, and Latinx theology. Women's experiences of sexism and subjugation led to the rise of feminist, womanist, and *mujerista* theology. People's experiences and contexts matter in how we do theology. Presently in a context of white, male, heterosexual, hegemonic understandings and expressions of Christian theology, understanding and exploring experiences of sexism, racism, homophobia, classism, ableism as intersecting categories that further lead to oppression and marginalization are essential facets of doing theology. We often tend to think of individuals' identities and lived experiences within separate categories of gender, race, sexual identity, and the like, but these categories are actually and essentially interrelated and intertwined. In reality, we cannot separate these categories from each other, as they all intersect to further discriminate against, oppress, and subjugate the other. Part of the task of intersectional theology is to recognize and understand our own lived experiences in order to understand God's presence in our lives and to begin to rethink theology from the perspectives of marginalized voices. Hearing many diverse voices and experiences from the margins will help all of us in understanding God's presence in our world.

Our own personal stories highlight some of the places where intersections of gender, race, nation, sexual identity, age, social class, and religion have been particularly salient for us. These profound moments of awareness of the dynamics of difference, power, oppression, and liberation have shaped and continue to shape our theologies. Our similar/different stories suggest the value of both/and thinking for theology by making visible the ways intersections create different experiences that lead to rich and diverse theological understandings. Suffering as *han* and suffering within process theology are similar and yet not the same. Intersectional thinking allows us to embrace both without having to reduce them to sameness, and both can contribute to a more nuanced theology of suffering. Both notions are closely connected to our individual identities and stories, and yet we both benefit when we welcome the experiences and understandings of the other—without ignoring difference or flattening meaning to make us say the same thing.

Our individual biographies are contextualized within larger narratives—of family, of country, of Christianity—and within social institutions that situate us in different relationships to power. These individual experiences then lead us to our own distinctive theologizing that contributes to a larger, more multilayered understanding of God. These individual experiences, however, are not simply atomized into such small units that they are useless to conceptual thinking. Rather, by applying intersectional thinking, we gather all of the individual narratives and idiosyncratic identities and experiences into a multifaceted unity that is constituted by its original parts without subsuming their distinctiveness into an undifferentiated whole. Certainly, this complicates theology, but we believe it also brings theology closer to the realities at the heart of the theological enterprise and is richer and more descriptive than theological artifices that demand uniformity and agreement.

In the next chapter, we turn to the questions of intersectionality for theology. How can we be attentive to difference? How can we center lived experience and at the same time strive for larger understandings of the Divine? What does theology look like when it is done with attention to the intersections and a bias toward justice? Our stories hint at these answers. In the next chapter, we invite all of those who do theology to engage in this introspection and awareness as we imagine a fully intersectional theology.

QUESTIONS

1. How is your theology embedded in your personal history? What life stories give rise to particular theological understandings?

2. What do the idiosyncrasies and particularities of your story have to offer to the larger narrative of Christian theology?

3. Write your own stories and biographies. How are your stories both/and experiences? How are your stories a story of intersectionality?

4. Compare and contrast your stories with Grace's and Susan's. How do the similarities and differences give rise to nuanced theological understandings? What do these stories share? What does each in its specificity offer to the larger Christian story? What is the value of holding all of these stories in mind at the same time?

5. The Korean term *han* was introduced in this chapter. Can you resonate with this term *han*? Have you experienced *han* in your own life?

6. Process theology invites us to view God differently from the classical theological perspective. Is this helpful in your own theological reflections on God?

7. How do your life experiences and stories help you develop a theology? In particular an intersectional theology?

3.

Intersectionality as Theological Method

As a theological method, intersectionality presumes that each of us does theology from a social location that has influence (of which we are sometimes aware and sometimes not) on our theologies. Rather than a call for a single, internally consistent and coherent system, intersectional theology is a call for intentional and deep attention to the ways social location affects theologies, a recognition of the impossibility of universalizing theologies, and an embrace of multiple theological perspectives as necessary and desirable in moving toward more inclusive theologies that capture the breadth and diversity of human encounter with the Divine. An intersectional theology recognizes that each of us exists in differing relationships to power and hierarchy based on gender, race, class, nation, sexual identity, ability, age, and other forms of social difference. We simultaneously experience advantage and disadvantage based on the intersections of these identities within interlocking systems of oppression, and these complex and nuanced distinctions play an important role in how each of us does theology. Our identities and experiences are never removed from the theologies we produce. There is always some context in which we do our theology, and theology exists in context. This fact of existence offers both limitations and possibilities for our theologizing. On the one hand, we cannot produce theologies for which we claim universal applicability; on the other, we can only produce the theologies that we do from our social locations, and so each of us has something significant to add to the whole of Christian theology. Without each of our contributions, the whole is less adequate, less descriptive of the entirety of theological possibility. So, for example, in her overview of feminist Christologies, Lisa Isherwood draws from the diverse traditions of womanist, Native American, mujerista, African, Asian, queer, Latin American, disability, and postcolonial feminist theologians to offer a complex landscape of christological perspectives—from the Christ of the ghettos to Eco-Sophia to Jesus as the Corn Mother—tying the embodiment of Christ to the embodiment of women across their social differences.[1]

In the field of biblical criticism, Elisabeth Schüssler Fiorenza draws from the work of Alicia Suskin Ostriker to suggest a "hermeneutics of indeterminacy" that "fosters plural readings."[2] She uses the story of the Syrophoenician woman as an example, offering numerous conflicting and simultaneously plausible interpretations of the story, ranging from the historical-critical placement of the story within early church disputes to the salvation-historical approach that allegorizes the story to the postcolonial approach that recognizes the ways the story has been used toward colonialist ends. She notes her own tradition-historical reading that situates the story in missionary beginnings, with the woman arguing against limiting the early church to Israel alone. She also points to Hisako Kinukawa's cultural-ethnic reading, which draws parallels between ethnic exclusion in the first-century world and in contemporary Japan. She then notes a sociohistorical reading of the story in terms of first-century Jewish class conflict, with Jesus expressing the resentments of the poor. Finally, she draws on Sharon Ringe's gender reading, arguing that the story is an attempt by the early church to put the best face on an unflattering story about Jesus. Quick to remind, however, that not all readings have equal value, Schüssler Fiorenza also calls for a "hermeneutics of evaluation" that gives value to interpretations based on their contribution to liberation. Its goal, she states, is "to unmask biblical texts and readings that foster an elite 'feminine,' racist, exclusivist, dehumanizing colonialist or Christian anti-Jewish inscription of cultural-religious identity."[3] Within this framework, biblical interpretation becomes an "argumentative, persuasive, and emancipatory praxis that destabilizes, proliferates, and energizes critical readings for liberation."[4]

We consider intersectional theology to be a "theology of indeterminacy." By that, we mean that intersectional theology does not seek to articulate ultimate truth claims but rather destabilizes fixed notions of theological truth by offering multiple and competing statements of

---

1. Lisa Isherwood, *Introducing Feminist Christologies* (Cleveland: Pilgrim, 2002).
2. Elisabeth Schüssler Fiorenza, *Sharing Her Word: Feminist Biblical Interpretation in Context* (Boston: Beacon, 1998), 106.
3. Schüssler Fiorenza, *Sharing Her Word*, 129.
4. Schüssler Fiorenza, *Sharing Her Word*, 129.

experiences and understandings across and within differences and evaluating those statements through a lens of justice. Furthermore, intersectional theology is a praxis that engages in actual work toward justice rooted in destabilized and intersectional understandings of individuals, institutional structures, and power. As Vivian May points out, intersectional approaches do not presume an underlying sameness but take seriously the realities of diverse ways of being and knowing.[5] She argues that intersectionality "underscores that a many-horizoned way of perceiving and a multifaceted, complex form of being is necessary." She emphasizes that this multidimensional approach recognizes that truths other than the dominant narratives have always existed but have often been rendered invisible by power asymmetries. Theologians, then, must learn to read multiplicities but without assimilating these diverse narratives into their own. Instead, we must embrace the "opaqueness and incomprehensibility" of the knowledges and stories of others in order to engage faithfully with people who differ from ourselves. This is particularly important as we relate across groups (between center and margin) and within groups who exist in differing relationships to various other margins.[6] May explains that this approach creates openness to engage authentically across differences without needing an assimilating sameness to underlie our diverse experiences, knowledges, and theologies. The struggle, she notes, is how to do this without falling back on narratives of sameness as the way to understanding. In other words, we must learn how to understand differences without turning them into sameness.

She suggests that to accomplish this goal, we must learn to "bracket"; in other words, we have to teach ourselves to participate in the logic of the claim; we have to enter the framework of others and resist the temptation to fold it into our own existing logics.[7] For theology, this means we must set aside the structures of dominant theologies and theological methods; indeed we may need to rupture them to be able to hear diverse and multiple voices. The dominant white male Eurocentric theology and method have been with us for the past 2,000 years and the welcoming of new voices from around the globe is now long overdue. In this way, as May suggests, we then depart from our "default frameworks and hegemonic imaginaries" and "take up 'bias' toward intersectional logics."[8] This in turn will allow creative theological voices to emerge and

---

5. Vivian May, *Pursuing Intersectionality, Unsettling Dominant Imaginaries* (New York: Routledge, 2015), 219.
6. May, *Pursuing Intersectionality*, 219.
7. May, *Pursuing Intersectionality*, 221.
8. May, *Pursuing Intersectionality*, 223.

unveil to us the complexities and multiplicities of theological sites and methods.

By this we mean that all theologies are not of equal value. As May argues, intersectionality as a theory and method is biased toward justice. Likewise, intersectional theology is also biased away from dominance and toward justice, and so we evaluate the worth of diverse theologies based on their ability to further the goals of liberation of all people. Often our social privilege is invisible to us, and so we may not thoroughly examine the ways we are influenced by our dominant statuses. Certainly, this "slippage" is one we see in theologies of liberation that focus solely on writers' subordinate identity without reference to the intersections of dominant identities. So when white feminists write without reference to race or womanists write without reference to sexual identity or *minjung* theologians write without reference to gender or queer theologians write without reference to social class, the value of that contribution is limited because it leaves the intersections of dominant identities uncontested and unexamined. The problem of unexamined power is particularly acute in many traditional theologies written by heterosexual white men who theologize as if their ideas exist outside a social context and the influence of their own gender, race, class, and sexual identity. As much as our intersectional theology welcomes diverse and competing perspectives, it also demands critical evaluation from the lens of liberation for all people across all differences.

This approach means that in many ways intersectional theology is a destabilizing theology. It reminds us of the power and asymmetries that make universalizing theologies impossible and undesirable. It brings the assumptions of dominant cultures into focus and undermines their claims to universality. It also highlights those at the margins and centers their voices as part of its bias toward justice. It disrupts the dominance of traditional theologies and demands epistemological bias toward the voices that normally would be sidelined or silenced in theological discourse. Intersectional theology asks us to accept the possibility of meaningfulness, even where we ourselves cannot understand it. It asks us to accept the limitations of our own worldviews and embrace the possibilities of multiplicity, simultaneity, and heterogeneity.

Intersectional theology thus builds on the work of feminist theology incorporating personal experiences and social location as essential methodological components. Early white feminist theologians such as Rosemary Radford Ruether, Letty Russell, and Elisabeth Schüssler Fiorenza centered women's experiences as a counter to dominant white male theologies. Women of color feminist theologians such as Delores

Williams and Ada Maria Isasi-Diaz developed womanist and *mujerista* theologies to capture the intersections of gender with race in theology. Intersectional theology, as we envision it, continues in that tradition of centering experience and expands attention to difference both across and within identity groups. With its wider inclusive lens of gender, race, sexual identity, social class, ability, age, and nation, intersectional theology brings the shifting and often invisible structures of power and privilege to the fore and demands attentiveness to social location and the simultaneity of subordinate and dominant identities in our theologizing. With its bias toward justice, in particular, intersectional theology calls us to prioritize the margins and ensure our theologizing moves us toward a more just world by disrupting dominant paradigms and destabilizing structures of power while envisioning a way forward toward God's reign of peace.

INTERSECTIONALITY'S QUESTIONS FOR THEOLOGY

How, then, might we imagine intersectionality as a method for theology? What questions would intersectionality have us ask?

Not surprisingly, powerful examples of intersectional theology come from womanist theologians. Monica Coleman defines womanist theology as "a response to sexism in black theology and racism in feminist theology."[9] Additionally, womanist theologian Kelly Brown Douglas reminds us that theologians must also include class and sexuality in their analysis. She writes that womanist scholars "must make clear that homophobia in any form is unacceptable, and that heterosexism must be eradicated as it is a part of the same interlocking systems of race, gender, and class oppression."[10] In her womanist queer theology, Pamela Lightsey reminds us that intersectional analysis is womanist theology's primary point of departure from traditional white Western theologies, and these intersectional understandings are essential for the very practical purpose of bringing about reconciliation and peace.[11] Also highlighting the ethical imperative of womanist theology, Stephanie Mitchem contends that "an ethical response is needed to race and class and gender and all other forms of oppressions. . . . This multiplication of injustices moves womanist ethicists into specific directions in order to address these problems:

---

9. Monica Coleman, *Making a Way out of No Way: A Womanist Theology* (Minneapolis: Fortress Press, 2008), 6.

10. Kelly Brown Douglas, *The Black Christ* (Maryknoll, NY: Orbis, 1994), 101.

11. Pamela Lightsey, *Our Lives Matter: A Womanist Queer Theology* (Eugene, OR: Pickwick, 2015), xix–xx.

there can be no hierarchy of oppressions, no addressing one and ignoring the other, if there is ever to be real justice."[12]

Marcella Althaus-Reid reminds us of the importance of intersectional thinking in her explication of indecent theology. Drawing from and critiquing Latin American liberation theology, she refuses the exclusion of sexuality from theologizing about liberation. An indecent theology, she explains, is a "theology which problematizes and undresses the mythical layers of multiple oppression in Latin America, a theology which, finding its point of departure at the crossroads of liberation theology and queer thinking, will reflect on economic and theological oppression with passion and imprudence. An indecent theology will question the traditional Latin American field of decency and order as it permeates and supports the multiple (ecclesiological, theological, political and amatory) structures of life in my country, Argentina, and in my continent."[13] She argues for a "contextual theology without exclusions."[14] She purposefully connects issues of race/ethnicity, gender, economics, colonialism, religion, and sexuality as inextricably intertwined within systems that maintain dominance and subordination, including traditional liberation theologies that omit analysis of sexuality. She calls instead for liberation theology to become "a permanent exercise of serious doubting in theology" that refuses colonial theology's "traditional androcentric methodology which tends to absorb and adapt the most radical elements that can arise from the margins."[15]

Intersectional theology challenges the dominance of traditional theological method and resists its co-opting tendencies that tend to dilute and gentrify intersectionality's radical demands. Intersectional theology's refusal to deny multiplicity dislocates traditional theology's search for singularity and disrupts its flattening and colonizing tendencies to negate difference and demand conformity.

For example, Asian American theologian Kwok Pui-lan's work in postcolonial feminist theology focuses on these intersections of gender, race, class, sexuality, and nation and centers the need for decolonization of the theological enterprise. Biblical scholars first turned to postcolonial theory in the mid-1990s to understand the colonial context from which many biblical stories emerged and were staged. The first published attempt to outline postcolonial biblical criticism was R. S. Sugirtharajah

---

12. Stephanie Mitchem, *Introducing Womanist Theology* (Maryknoll, NY: Orbis, 2002), 57–58.
13. Marcella Althaus-Reid, *Indecent Theology: Theological Perversions in Sex, Gender and Politics* (New York: Routledge, 2000), 2.
14. Althaus-Reid, *Indecent Theology*, 4.
15. Althaus-Reid, *Indecent Theology*, 5.

in his 1996 article in the *Asia Journal of Theology*.[16] Postcolonial biblical criticism challenges us to rethink the biblical texts and provokes us to read them in an entirely new perspective. It forces us to recognize the imperial powers that have existed and how imperial powers controlled religion and how it continues to do so today. Postcolonial thinking provided new language and ways of interpreting the Bible that spoke to the experiences of people around the globe who have endured colonialism and its lasting generational consequences.

Postcolonial theory entered theological discourse in the early 2000s focusing theological attention on empire building, colonialism, imperialism, and power. Kwok argues that a "postcolonial imagination"—"a desire, a determination, and a process of disengagement from the whole colonial syndrome, which takes many forms and guises"—is key for theological reflection as scholars grapple with the legacies of colonialism at the center of much theology.[17] Postcolonial analysis challenges not only colonial regimes and frameworks but also our potential complicity in reinscribing colonial legacies through knowledge production. Kwok's work is integral to an intersectional theology, as her work exemplifies the intersectional thinking that includes power, economics, women of color, sexuality, and empire building. Her postcolonial feminist theology explicates how global women suffer under capitalism, colonialism, racism, and poverty and how they engage theology as a form of resistance to empire. Kwok argues that all women should engage in postcolonial theology, including First World white women. Noting that colonizers and the colonized will have "different entry points, priorities of issues, accents, and inflections," she asserts that "not only do the colonized need to disengage from the colonial syndrome, the colonizers have to decolonize their minds and practices as well."[18] She quickly adds, "female subalterns who experience the intersection of oppressions in the most immediate and brutal way have epistemological privileges in terms of articulating a postcolonial feminist theology that will be more inclusive than others."[19] In other words, while all theologians have a responsibility to decolonize their minds and their work, theology must privilege the most subaltern whose experiences convey a greater inclusivity by virtue of their more comprehensive view of oppression and colonization.

Similarly, Korean theologian Chung Hyun Kyung offers an analysis

---

16. R. S. Sugirtharajah, "From Orientalist to Post-Colonial: Notes on Reading Practices," *Asia Journal of Theology* 10 (1): 20–27.

17. Kwok Pui-lan, *Postcolonial Imagination and Feminist Theology* (Louisville: Westminster John Knox, 2005), 2–3.

18. Kwok, *Postcolonial Imagination and Feminist Theology*, 127.

19. Kwok, *Postcolonial Imagination and Feminist Theology*, 127.

of economic poverty, globalization, and capitalism as a crucial perspective in how Asian women do theology. She intersects economic analysis with interreligious dialogue and indigenous spirituality. Her theological method of using such experiences of poverty, gender, and religious marginalization helps her to develop a syncretistic Asian feminist theology. She recognizes that one dimension of a societal issue affects another aspect and that these issues do intersect and must be taken seriously when one engages in liberative theology. Chung writes, "When poverty strikes Third World people, the ones who suffer the most are women and children. They are also the majority of the population. When there are no material resources for survival, and many poor men have already lost their wills to continue their lives, most Third World women do not even have the luxury to give up their lives."[20] Economy and issues of poverty and gender are at the forefront of many Asian women's lives. These issues dictate how they manage their daily lives and the future of their children's lives. From this intersecting perspective of gender, economics, and race/ethnicity, many Asian women view their religions and how they live out their spirituality. And in most cases, they end up developing a syncretistic Asian feminist theology that will address the issues of poverty, patriarchy, and marginalization so that they will survive.

Chung continues to argue that Asian women are complex beings and are not one-dimensional. "Like black women," she writes, "we are Asian women all the time. We cannot compartmentalize aspects of our struggle. Our struggle is a struggle for wholeness."[21] Here she illustrates the interrelated dimensions of one's identity and emphasizes that no single aspect of identity defines Asian women. Rather, the totality of the intersectional lives that Asian women inhabit describes their lives.

Patrick S. Cheng is a gay Chinese American theologian who examines the concept of sin and highlights that the multiple identities of individuals who live at the "intersections of race, gender, sexual orientation, age, and other categories" all help in our understanding of sin.[22] Cheng recognizes that as an Asian American gay man he is marginalized in the white lesbian, gay, bisexual world and then further erased and ostracized by the heterosexual Asian American context. All these multiple sites of identity and intersections need to be taken into consideration when examining theological doctrines of grace, sin, and humanity. One

---

20. Chung Hyun Kyung, *Struggle to Be the Sun Again: Introducing Asian Women's Theology* (Maryknoll, NY: Orbis, 1990), 23.

21. Chung, *Struggle to Be the Sun Again*, 35.

22. Patrick S. Cheng, "Rethinking Sin and Grace for LGBT People Today," in *Sexuality and the Sacred: Sources for Theological Reflection*, 2nd edition, ed. Marvin M. Ellison and Kelly Brown Douglas (Louisville: Westminster John Knox, 2010), 115.

cannot ignore these multiple sites, as they contribute to how we develop theological teachings and doctrines.

As these examples demonstrate, social location matters. Attending to the intersections matters. Theologies are reflections of these social locations and intersections, and an intersectional theology demands theologians' attentiveness to them. What, then, are the questions intersectionality demands theologians ask of themselves?

HOW DOES MY OWN SOCIAL LOCATION AFFECT HOW I LOOK AT ISSUES?

We need look no further than the history of theology from the early church to the present to see the impact of ignoring social location. Traditional theologies are replete with examples of the assumption of the mythical norm behind theological ideas. By ignoring social location, white, male, heterosexual theologians have accepted and perpetuated, for example, notions of God as male, to the extent that in 1992, the Southern Baptist Convention declared, "the revelation of God as Father is central and essential to Trinitarian faith."[23] In 2008, Southern Baptist professor Terry Wilder explained, "God clearly expects to be understood primarily in masculine terms."[24] Similarly, the understanding of sin in the garden of Eden arises from men's experiences. For centuries, male interpreters understood the primary sin of Adam to be pride, with self-sacrifice as its solution, but, as feminist interpreters in the 1960s noted, pride is hardly a problem for most women; rather, self-abnegation is a greater risk. So in her 1960 essay "The Human Situation: A Feminine View," Valerie Saiving argued that women's sins "are better suggested by such terms as triviality, distractibility, and diffuseness; lack of an organizing center or focus; dependence on others for one's sense of self-definition; tolerance at the expense of standards of excellence; inability to respect the boundaries of privacy; sentimentality, gossipy sociability, and mistrust of reason—in short, underdevelopment or negation of the self."[25] Unfortunately, even as white women theologians began to question the assumptions of maleness behind most traditional theology, they did not often note their own social locations with regard to race, sexual identity, or nation, identities within which they were often privileged.

23. Southern Baptist Convention, "Resolution on God the Father," https://tinyurl.com/y82h9fwx.
24. Terry L. Wilder, "God—the Father," *SBCLife*, August 1, 2008, https://tinyurl.com/y85nv934.
25. Valerie Saiving, "The Human Situation: A Feminine View," *The Journal of Religion* 40, no. 2 (1960): 109.

A truly intersectional theology will pay attention to all of these intersections of identity, exploring how both subordinate and dominant identities at these intersections affect the ways we all do theology.

The doctrine of sin has usually been viewed as one-dimensional. Augustine had a tremendous influence on the doctrine of sin by suggesting "original sin." Augustine argues, "Man's nature ... was created at first faultless and without any sin."[26] Human beings were not created with sin, but once they rebelled in the garden of Eden by eating from the tree of knowledge of good and evil, they committed sin, and it is transmitted by human generation. The cause of this fall is blamed on the act of Eve who tempted Adam to eat of the fruit from the tree of knowledge. This view understands sin as an act of transgression committed against God. This has long been the traditional view of sin in church tradition. However, as other theological voices have emerged, especially feminist theology, we have begun to see that sin is complex and can be understood from multiple sites.

Feminist theologian Joy McDougall points out that there is a man-made "feminization of sin" that has been disguised as part of the fallen state of humanity. It has led to the divine order of subordinating women under male authority.[27] As a result, sin gets defined within patriarchy, and women are always viewed as subordinate to men due to male theological understandings of original sin. In light of this patriarchal view of sin, intersectional theology forces us to redefine sin and take it out of its invisible and unexamined patriarchal context. Intersectional theology reminds us that sin happens in multiple political, economic, religious, racial, and gender sites. Sin is not something that is committed against God (the vertical understanding of sin), but rather it is committed against other human beings (through sinful structures of patriarchy, capitalism, heteronormativity, imperialism, and white supremacy), and it is collective as well as individual. Furthermore, we are not just sinful against one another but also against God's creation as we continue to pollute, destroy, and subjugate the earth. Intersectional theology challenges us to remove ourselves from the patriarchal notion of sin and to create just structures and to work toward justice within ourselves and our communities and in creation.

---

26. Augustine, *On Nature and Grace* III.1; Fathers of the Church.

27. Joy McDougall, "The Bondage of the Eye/I? A Transnational Feminist Wager for Reimagining the Doctrine of Sin," in *Reimagining with Christian Doctrines*, ed. Grace Ji-Sun Kim and Jenny Daggers (New York: Palgrave Macmillan, 2014), 107.

HOW IS THIS THEOLOGY CONTEXTUALIZED?

We recognize that theology is done within a context, and for feminist thinkers context becomes an important part of theological method. Context provides the backdrop and circumstances in which we experience God. Lisa Isherwood notes that context is not simply one's individual identity. Rather, she explains, "Context refers to social location and is a category that can be shared by others in one's group who will suffer the same restrictions because of it." Context is also intersectional and includes positions of both subordination and domination. Isherwood adds that contextual theology requires "multiple levels of analysis and a many-layered pattern of resistance."[28] Mercy Amba Oduyoye points to African women's Christology as arising from a context of suffering at the intersections of colonialism, poverty, and gender. She points out that African women have employed specifically liberative cultural paradigms to articulate their belief in Jesus. Rarely does their vocabulary focus on Christ; their words are almost always about Jesus. Oduyoye explains, "Jesus is the brother or kin who frees women from the domination of inhuman husbands. Women relate more easily to the Christ who knew hunger, thirst, and homelessness, and see Jesus as oppressed by the culture of his own people. Jesus the liberator is a paradigm for the critique of culture that most African women theologians do."[29]

WHAT IS THE HISTORY OF MY INTERPRETIVE COMMUNITY, AND HOW IS IT INFLUENCING MY INTERPRETATION?

If we come from a colonized context, for example, that will influence our hermeneutics and how we apply Scripture to our present context. If we are poor, our socioeconomic context will shape our readings of how the rich and poor live today. Our community identities also influence the questions of theology and often rank priorities, even within the liberatory church. Musimbi R. A. Kanyoro points out how the African context of colonialism and Western imperialism creates theological struggle as African women face both cultural expectations and the needs of daily living. She points out that even within liberation traditions, women's issues are often "trivialized in favor of 'larger' issues such as national liberation,

---

28. Lisa Isherwood, *Liberating Christ* (Cleveland: Pilgrim, 1999), 16–17.
29. Mercy Amba Oduyoye, "Jesus Christ," in *Hope Abundant: Third World and Indigenous Women's Theology*, ed. Kwok Pui-lan (Maryknoll, NY: Orbis, 2010), 168.

famine, disease, war, and poverty." Within that context, then, individual women's acts of resistance to injustice in the church "are seen as immoral rather than prophetic."[30] In other words, within this interpretive community, women's issues are positioned as secondary, and sometimes as antithetical, to the (male) community's focus on broader national issues, and women's advocacy for gender perspectives becomes perceived as sinful rather than central to a theology that encompasses broader human experience across gender as well as nation and race.

Ivone Gebara notes, "What happens is that a woman's action is always limited by the male way of understanding the world and organizing the different social institutions."[31] This means, she continues, that when women do achieve power—institutional or interpretive—they often end up leaving feminist principles behind to survive in the patriarchal hierarchy (or being fired for refusing to assimilate to institutional thinking). Religious institutions, she warns, are able to absorb a certain amount of reform without transformation and so continue to reproduce "'North American-centric' domination."[32]

Randy Woodley, a Native American theologian, reminds us what happened to Native American land under the idea of conquest. He writes, "The historical metanarrative of the *American Dream*, which is accompanied by notions of equality for all, has been used to smooth over historically inconvenient truths and awkward facts of tragedy that have befallen America's indigenous peoples at the willing hands of America's settler population."[33] Native land was confiscated by white European settlers and the genocide began against Native Americans.

Woodley puts into perspective the truth about American history. He continues, "The truth is, the country that most Americans hold so dear is mostly stolen property. Part of the purpose of the American Dream's familiar narrative is to create a 'pseudo-place.' The pseudo-place of social location is held in place of real land. The social location acts as a placeholder for real land. In turn, the placeholder of social location deeply influences an American theology of the land."[34] This isn't Christianity but goes against Christian teachings and values. Therefore, we cannot

---

30. Musimbi R. A. Kanyoro, "Engendered Communal Theology: African Women's Contribution to Theology in the Twenty-First Century," in *Hope Abundant: Third World and Indigenous Women's Theology*, ed. Kwok Pui-lan (Maryknoll, NY: Orbis, 2010), 21.

31. Ivone Gebara, "A Feminist Theology of Liberation: A Latin American Perspective with a View Toward the Future," in *Hope Abundant: Third World and Indigenous Women's Theology*, ed. Kwok Pui-lan (Maryknoll, NY: Orbis, 2010), 56–57.

32. Gebara, "A Feminist Theology of Liberation," 56–57.

33. Randy S. Woodley, *Shalom and the Community of Creation: An Indigenous Vision* (Grand Rapids: Eerdmans, 2012), 131.

34. Woodley, *Shalom and the Community of Creation*, 131.

continue on the false claim that America is built on Christian values when it is rather built on colonialism, genocide, conquest, and a distortion of the Christian faith under false pretenses of missiology. White euro-Christians had a sense of superiority over Native Americans and this legitimated whatever horrible acts they committed against Native Americans in the name of God. Traditional missiology gave conquering settlers theological justification for taking the lands of native peoples and remains a central viewpoint in ongoing efforts to convert Native Americans and maintain the legacies of conquest. Intersectional theology invites us to reexamine this missiological history and its ongoing impacts on indigenous people and communities.

AM I USING SINGLE-AXIS THINKING?

The recognition that there are multiple axes of thinking widens our scope of critical reflection, learning, and theological reflection. If we fall into single-axis thinking, we flatten diversity within groups and ignore the myriad ways intersecting oppressions shape experience. For example, an edited volume on trans theology offers multiple exciting and new ways to imagine theologies from transgender perspectives, and yet writers give almost no thought to, for example, how intersections with race shape trans experience, despite the fact that trans women of color are at much greater risk of violent death than white trans women. How might this intersection offer a different perspective to trans theology? Likewise, many feminist theologies ignore gender identity and overlook the ways being at home in one's assigned gender offers certain privileging in the doing of theology.

HOW IS MY THINKING ABOUT THIS ISSUE BOTH/AND?

In the West, much of our thinking and understanding of concepts and even our understanding of time is linear, with a distinct beginning point and an end. But in the East, time and understanding are more entangled, intertwined, and nonlinear. Sometimes they become circular, and time itself is entangled and becomes a both/and and not necessarily a linear concept. Such a different outlook on the world reminds us that both/and is a much greater possibility and widens our perception of the world and enlarges our critical thinking. Both/and thinking requires we imagine the subjects of our theologizing in all of their complexity. Mary McClintock Fulkerson notes that in the contesting of terms like "woman" and "gender," "The point is not to lose the subject 'woman,' but to change the subject in the sense that the complex production of multiple identities becomes basic to our thinking."[35] Furthermore, both Asian and African feminist theologians call us to openness to multi-religious thinking. Mercy Oduyoye contends that "Christian exclusiveness is in large measure not biblical and must therefore not be allowed to become an obstacle in the multi-religious communities of Africa."[36] In this version of both/and thinking, we are challenged to reach beyond Christian exclusiveness (as well as our social location within gender, race, sexuality, and other identities) to include the histories and insights of other religious traditions.

We see how syncretism has played a role in the development of Christianity and even its doctrine. For example, Christian holidays such as Christmas and Easter are rooted in paganism. The Bible offers no mention of the exact date of the birth of Jesus in the Gospel narratives. In the early church, some believers circulated "heretical" teachings that Jesus was not a full human being. To counter this heresy, the church recognized that having a day to celebrate the birthday of Jesus and show that he was a human being was important. Midwinter festivals proved to be a good choice to celebrate the birth of Jesus. December 21 is the winter solstice, which is the shortest day of the year. Thus the day the sun is being born can be also viewed as when Christ is also born. This example of incorporating pagan festivities within Christian practices demonstrates that syncretism is not new in the church.

In fact, as we understand Jesus Christ as the wisdom of God, then we also see syncretism influencing our Christologies. Many scholars have shown that the biblical and apocryphal *Hokmah*/Sophia was a syncretistic understanding from the Egyptian goddess Isis.[37] This syncretistic understanding of the doctrine of Jesus Christ is particularly helpful to feminist theologians today, as it offers a mode of valuing women and women's contributions by affirming wider visions of gender in our constructions of God and Christ. Additionally, we see the value of syncretism in the contributions of Asian American Christology, which brings together Christian interpretations with understandings from inherited syncretistic cultures and religions such as Shamanism, Buddhism, and Confucianism.

---

35. Mary McClintock Fulkerson, *Changing the Subject: Women's Discourses and Feminist Theology* (Minneapolis: Fortress Press, 1994), 7.

36. Mercy Amba Oduyoye, "Jesus Christ," in *Hope Abundant: Third World and Indigenous Women's Theology*, ed. Kwok Pui-lan (Maryknoll, NY: Orbis, 2010), 181.

37. Grace Ji-Sun Kim, *The Grace of Sophia: A Korean North American Women's Christology* (Cleveland: Pilgrim, 2002), 81.

HOW IS POWER AT WORK IN THE HISTORY OF THIS IDEA?

Management theorist Mary Parker Follett identified two forms of power: "power-over," the ability to force or coerce, and "power-with," the ability to work with others to accomplish goals.[38] Feminists have added "power-to" to our understandings of power. This is the power of agency, the ability to act.[39] Traditionally, the West has had power over the East, and similarly men have had power over women; whites over people of color; straight over LGBTQ. Intersections of identities complicate the workings of power further, creating ever more nuanced hierarchies and distributing power in greater degree the closer one approximates the mythical norm. While resistance movements often still exercise power-over within groups, these movements against oppression have often tried intentionally to move toward models of power-to and power-with. Power works in these ways, not only as raw coercive strength, but also as language and ideology. Disrupting inequality and the unequal distribution of power and access requires examination of the ideologies that inform systems of oppression, including theology.

So, for example, Lisa Isherwood examines the tradition of Christologies and finds that "The tradition is male, white, Western, and elitist. The Christ of faith who rises from this landscape is not altogether a liberative figure." She suggests that this tradition of Christ has resulted in "changing the story from that of transforming praxis and liberation to personal salvation." While this Christ, she suggests, may have led some people to live good lives, on the whole, this image instead has "been used to underpin conquest and genocide." She explains, "The Christ who was born of a virgin, lived dispensing God's grace, died for the forgiveness of sins, and rose again in glory is the foundation stone for pain, suffering, and abuse of others."[40]

What Isherwood points to is a christological tradition rooted in white, Western patriarchy that is rarely examined for the ways it reproduces and distributes power to maintain the dominance of the status quo. An intersectional theology will scrutinize how power is deployed in theological ideas, texts, and applications with particular attention to issues of dominant and subordinate identities and interlocking systems of oppression. Again, Isherwood points out, "The patriarchal imposition of power-over has caused suffering throughout the world, and liberation theolo-

---

38. Mary P. Follett, "Dynamic Administration: The Collected Papers of Mary Parker Follett," ed. E. M. Fox and L. Urwick (London: Pitman Publishing, 1940).

39. Pamela Pansardi, "Power To and Power Over: Two Distinct Concepts of Power?" *Journal of Political Power* 5, no. 1 (2012): 73–89.

40. Lisa Isherwood, *Liberating Christ* (Cleveland: Pilgrim, 1999), 137.

gians first reflected upon this application of power. However, they were slower to consider how the power within systems of religion adversely affected people and possibly even slower to admit that the same power structures were in place in secular and religious systems."[41]

In contrast, she says, the power of the embodied Christ narrative is to be found precisely in the arena traditional theologies often disparage—the power of the erotic. She explains, "This raw, dynamic energy that exists within and between us is the power of Christ, the power that can burst out and transform" and warns the "impotency of metaphysics is always a danger in Christian theology." She points to the church's long history of fear and hatred of embodied power, noting how Eve is presented as an example of the danger of embodiment. Rather, she argues, through embodiment and intimate connection people can move beyond their limitations into true transformation and empowerment.[42]

The doctrine of the resurrection of the body and eschatology has been problematic for some feminist theologians. It has been a doctrine to support "escape" from our bodies or it has affirmed loathing of our bodies. The doctrine of the "resurrection of the body" has been used to reinforce that our bodies do not matter and that the body of the world to come is what really matters. We see this over and over again when our bodies become sick or ill or we become disabled, and we try to mitigate our present suffering by affirming that our present bodies will become new in the next world. Feminist theologian Cynthia Rigby reminds us that the "resurrection of the body" as an escapist notion must be rejected.[43]

The church has often framed suffering as redemptive, but intersectional theology demands we ask if we can truly imagine that suffering is redemptive in light of disabled bodies. What questions do disabled bodies raise for notions of redemptive suffering? What does suffering redeem us from anyway? What do we mean to suggest in saying that suffering is somehow acceptable to God or, perhaps, even required by God?

The church has shamed certain "bodies" such as women's bodies, disabled bodies, trans bodies, black bodies, poor bodies, and brown bodies. We need to move toward a redemptive understanding of our bodies by rejecting white, able, heterosexual male bodies as the norm. We need to move away from "escapism" and embrace the beautiful bodies that God has given to us and understand that even our bodies are intersectional, complicated, and multifaceted. The doctrine of bodily resurrection has

---

41. Isherwood, *Liberating Christ*, 145.
42. Isherwood, *Liberating Christ*, 145–47.
43. Cynthia Rigby, "Chains Fall Off: The Resurrection of the Body and Our Healing from Shame," in *Reimagining with Christian Doctrines*, ed. Grace Ji-Sun Kim and Jenny Daggers (New York: Palgrave Macmillan, 2014), 51.

been used to bring shame on our bodies, but a reworking of this notion to liberate our bodies from shame is long overdue.

Perhaps queer bodies provide another intersectional way forward. Rather than imagining queer bodies in need of redemption from their queerness, perhaps we can imagine queer bodies as redemptive in their rejection of heteronormativity. Particularly when we engage intersectional thinking, we can imagine queer bodies of color or disabled queer bodies as themselves issuing a challenge to white, patriarchal, able-bodied heteronormativity.

HOW DOES THIS IDEA REPRODUCE OR CHALLENGE INEQUITIES?

An intersectional theology must be self-aware, examining its own oppressive and liberatory possibilities. It must seek to challenge injustices in historical theologies, as well as in its own worldview. And it must go beyond simply identifying inequities; it must offer solutions for addressing injustice. For example, Sharon A. Bong argues that liberatory theologies must be embodied. For her, Asian theologies are "premised on the historical and material conditions of specific Asian communities and articulated from their positions of marginality *and* agency," with a specific goal of reclaiming the centrality of the body, especially for Asian women. This approach, she explains, effects three "doctrinal transgressions" through its challenge to traditional Christian theologies: it rejects the church's denigration of the body through duality and asceticism; it rejects a disembodied Godhead and centers the "humanization of God in the body of Christ who suffers, resists, and heals"; and it rejects theology's abstracting tendencies in favor of a praxis that moves the world toward greater justice and sustainability.[44] In centering the body in the experiences of Asians and Asian women in particular, Bong challenges the traditional abstraction and rejection of the body by Christian theology that undergirds the marginalization and subordination of women and women's greater vulnerability to intersecting oppressions. In contrast, she offers a restructuring of theological and social relations that recognizes "the body is the spirit" and demands "compassionate identification and solidarity with the marginalized."[45]

Dominant eschatologies, for example, often reproduce and maintain inequalities. With their focus on the "sweet by and by," they encourage

---

44. Sharon A. Bong, "The Suffering Christ and the Asian Body," in *Hope Abundant: Third World and Indigenous Women's Theology*, ed. Kwok Pui-lan (Maryknoll, NY: Orbis, 2010), 186.
45. Bong, "The Suffering Christ and the Asian Body," 190–91.

subordinated peoples to accept their status in return for the promise of equity and justice in God's future community. Traditional eschatologies also typically delineate between the "saved" and the "lost"—the insiders and outsiders, the cosmological winners and losers. Intersectional theology challenges the dominating tendencies of such exclusionary eschatological notions by questioning the assumption that some are God's favored and some are not. In contrast, intersectional theology also raises possibilities for imagining a present eschatology—an in-breaking of God's community of love and justice in the present.

WHAT DOES INTERSECTIONAL THINKING DO WHEN APPLIED TO THIS PROBLEM?

Lisa Isherwood points out that liberation theologies cannot stop with ideas; they must create action. In fact, the paradigm for liberation theologies is praxis, a process of action, reflection, and more action. Isherwood notes, "This theology does not allow its practitioners to wallow in safe, contemplative bliss. They have to face harsh reality and attempt to change it. . . . The notion that salvation has a history, the one we are living now, means that Christians have a responsibility to shape that history according to the liberative ideals of Jesus."[46] Applying intersectional thinking to theological problems means moving from reflection to action, from injustice to justice. As we do intersectional theology, we must imagine how applying intersectional thinking to problems will move us forward toward justice.

What would this application, mean, for example, if we asked intersectional theological questions of reproductive justice? An intersectional understanding could help us complicate our thinking about reproductive issues as both/and. For example, fetal life is both inherently valuable and fetal life is not personhood. This shift moves discussion from the either/or of valuing either the fetus or the woman to understanding that both have value, and that discussions of abortion are about choosing between two important and competing values. Intersectional thinking further complicates the issue by forcing us to reckon with the impact of gender, race, and social class on reproductive justice. Which women have access to contraception and abortion? What social contexts shape and limit women's abilities to control their own reproduction? How do our understandings of "life" need to shift, grow, and become more nuanced

---

46. Isherwood, *Liberating Christ*, 17.

in light of these intersections? How do these complicated notions shape the church's response to women's reproductive needs?

HOW DOES THIS WORK SHIFT THE CENTER?

Intersectional theology challenges the center and the status quo. It shifts the center and allows room for multiple centers that co-exist and empower each other. Within traditional theologies, the mythical norm occupies the center. Whiteness, maleness, able-bodiedness, Westernness, heterosexuality—these all provide the lens, experience, and dominant narrative for traditional theologies. Intersectional theology recognizes that who occupies the center matters. For example, Kelly Brown Douglas moves black bodies to the center of her theologizing in *Stand Your Ground: Black Bodies and the Justice of God*. In so doing, she articulates parallels between the crucifixion of Jesus and the killing of Trayvon Martin by a white man who used Florida's stand-your-ground law to claim self-defense. Drawing from James Cone's assertion that the crucifixion was a lynching, Douglas argues that Jesus identified with the victims of "the lynched/crucified class."[47] In response to the question, "Where was God when Trayvon was slain?," Douglas asserts, "What we know for sure is that God was not a part of the crucifying mob. Thus, on the night when Trayvon was slain, God was where life was crying out to be free from the crucifying death of stand-your-ground culture."[48] By shifting the center of theology away from the mythical norm and to black bodies, Douglas offers a new and important perspective for understanding and addressing collective and social sin, racism, and violence.

HOW DO I READ THIS ISSUE AGAINST THE GRAIN?

The challenge of reading against the grain asks us to reject the traditional, expected readings in favor of the surprising and disruptive. Queer theology offers one lens for reading theology against the grain. Susannah Cornwall suggests that queer theology is theology that is at odds with the norm. She explains that queer theologies "have the potential to stand over against constrictive, limiting ideologies" as a "proactive *unknowing* about God." She concludes, "since theology points to a God who is not fully known, part of becoming like that God is being prepared to give up

---

47. Kelly Brown Douglas, *Stand Your Ground: Black Bodies and the Justice of God* (Maryknoll, NY: Orbis, 2016), 174.
48. Douglas, *Stand Your Ground*, 203.

part of what we believe we know about ourselves as humans."⁴⁹ Reading against the grain recognizes that traditional theologies have been constructed primarily by heterosexual, white, Western men and reflect their experiences, interests, and benefit. Reading theology against the grain causes us to question the hidden assumptions of race, gender, sexuality, nation, and other forms of difference in traditional theologies and offer nonnormative readings that are partial, contradictory, and conflicting.

When we read the major theologians in our Christian tradition, we may recognize that they are mostly white, Western men, such as Augustine, Aquinas, Anselm, Luther, Calvin, and Schleiermacher. As we reread some of their writing against the grain, we recognize that these texts were written within the theologians' specific context, culture, and society (including their own privileged social locations as white, Western, and male), and we must recognize the resultant limitations of their theologizing, which means, while we can learn from their work, we cannot apply their theological teaching and doctrines for all time. For example, Anselm's theory of atonement uses the language of serfs and lords that was common for his time period, and his readers would have readily recognized this language. For us today, however, this is not our common language or our worldview. We recognize that Anselm's theory is situated in his own particular context and patriarchal understanding of the world. Reading his writings against the grain will help us weed out negative understandings of women in his works. Similarly, as we reject Luther's anti-Semitism, we must also reject his sexism. We do not excuse it as a reflection of his historical setting, but we name it as problematic, and we trace and condemn its history and influence that continues in the church to the present. Reading against the grain challenges us to ask hard questions of theological texts in order to understand how those texts are shaped by gender, race, class, sexuality, and other forms of difference in ways that support existing power structures and how those texts have been and continue to be used to reinforce the dominant social order.

WHAT DO OTHER VOICES SAY? ARE THEY FULLY INTERSECTIONAL?

Our own perspectives, while important contributors to the theological dialogue, are limited by our experiences and social locations. Therefore, intersectional theology requires our engagement with other diverse

---

49. Susannah Cornwall, "Apophasis and Ambiguity: The 'Unknowingness' of Transgender," in *Trans/Formations*, ed. Marcella Althaus-Reid and Lisa Isherwood (London: SCM, 2009), 16–17.

voices from multiple and often competing locations. In particular, we must listen for other voices in solidarity toward social justice. Kwok Pui-lan argues, "Since globalization and the current form of Empire are de-centered and de-territorialized, transnational and intercultural alliances among marginalized women doing theology are necessary."[50]

HOW DO I HOLD MULTIPLE AND COMPETING VOICES IN MIND AT THE SAME TIME?

Multiple and differing voices will enrich our dialogue with one another rather than be a distraction. These diverse voices will help enliven the work of theology as it deepens our knowledge and helps us move toward a liberative theology. For example, Hyo-Dong Lee attempts to bring in the Asian concept of Qi or Spirit into the Christian discussion of the Spirit. He offers an exciting comparative discussion of Confucianism and Daoism with Western concepts of Geist and Spirit. Lee adds to the emerging discussion of panentheistic Christian theologies of God's presence in the universe.[51]

Linda Thomas, a womanist theologian, argues for an African spirituality in Christian theological pneumatology. She attempts to look at the ways the "Spirit in African American churches fused elements of African cosmologies with white Christianity to form a unique religion with a notion of the Spirit that sits within an orthodox Christian framework with distinctive features."[52] Black women connect African cosmology with Christianity to develop a pneumatology that is liberative for black women. When Africans migrate or move, they take their religion with them, and thus, even if they convert to Christianity, they do not abandon their traditional religion. Thomas writes, "Black women drew on a dual system of spirituality to deal with their radical marginality and move toward survival and quality of life. On the one hand, there was African cosmology, where freedom or justice is linked to well-being, thriving, good health, and flourishing as the basic goals of the good life."[53] They are aware of the Spirit with its elaborate cosmologies that include and involve multiple divinities and ancestors. They also understand that it is

---

50. Kwok Pui-lan, "Introduction," in *Hope Abundant: Third World and Indigenous Women's Theology*, ed. Kwok Pui-lan (Maryknoll, NY: Orbis, 2010), 9.

51. For further discussion please read Hyo-Dong Lee, *Spirit, Qi, and the Multitude: A Comparative Theology for the Democracy of Creation* (New York: Fordham University Press, 2014).

52. Linda Thomas, "The Holy Spirit and Black Women: A Womanist Perspective," in *Christian Doctrines for Global Gender Justice*, ed. Jenny Daggers and Grace Ji-Sun Kim (New York: Palgrave Macmillan, 2015), 73–78.

53. Thomas, "The Holy Spirit and Black Women," 77.

the Spirit that guides and empowers them. Rather than feeling a need to reject one tradition in favor of another, these theologians draw from diverse traditions and hold multiple voices in mind at the same time, thereby expanding the possibilities for complex understandings of Spirit.

AM I ACTING IN COLLUSION WITH DOMINATING POWERS?

In her description of "diasporic imagination," Kwok Pui-lan warns that feminist theologians must be "mindful of the complicit roles women have played in spawning the myths of origins and upholding the rituals and celebrations that put them in a subordinate position."[54] She also reminds us that as a Christian theologian, she must pay attention to the ways anti-Jewish and anti-Semitic tendencies can appear in Christian feminist theologies.[55] Intersectional theology must be mindful of the possibilities of collusion, against one's own group and against other subordinate groups. Intersectional theology will seek out both manifestations of internalized oppression and horizontal hostility and harms against others. Intersectional theologies will not sacrifice justice for others in order to succeed in obtaining justice for some, which is no real justice at all. Rather, intersectional theologies will examine possibilities for collusion and co-optation and resist the assimilating tendencies of dominant powers. Kwok Pui-lan argues that "not only do the colonized need to disengage from the colonial syndrome, the colonizers have to decolonize their minds and practices as well."[56] She reminds us, "The struggle for gender justice, for those without safe water to drink and adequate food to put on the table, cannot be fought primarily at the cultural-symbolic level, without simultaneously attending to sociopolitical struggles."[57] An intersectional theology must avoid collusion with dominant powers in order to act fully on behalf of justice.

At this moment in the United States, we are seeing an unprecedented collusion of traditional evangelical theologies with present political powers. White evangelical voters overwhelmingly supported a twice-divorced man who bragged about groping women and who claimed he had never asked anyone for forgiveness. They rationalized that his likelihood of appointing conservative judges who would overturn *Roe*

---

54. Kwok Pui-lan, *Postcolonial Imagination and Feminist Theology* (Louisville: Westminster John Knox, 2005), 48.
  55. Kwok, *Postcolonial Imagination and Feminist Theology*, 49.
  56. Kwok, *Postcolonial Imagination and Feminist Theology*, 127.
  57. Kwok, *Postcolonial Imagination and Feminist Theology*, 130.

v. Wade and uphold other conservative political ideologies outweighed any need for him to be personally moral and ethical himself. In another shocking moment, one political actor supported a senatorial candidate accused of molesting a teenager by excusing the candidate's propensity for teenage girls as no more than the relationship between Mary and Joseph. Intersectional theology demands a critique of theologies that justify the abuse of others, widening of gaps of inequality, discrimination against groups of people, and disregard for the suffering of others. Intersectional theology necessitates resistance to dominating powers. It reminds us that our theologies must never be tools of governmental power, even when that power purports to enact our theological wishes.

HOW DOES MY THINKING RADICALLY REFORM THEOLOGY?

Intersectional thinking radically changes how we think about theology. Theology can no longer be viewed as monochromatic but rather becomes a dynamic enterprise with multifaceted viewpoints, perspectives, and understandings. We can no longer approach theology as a singular voice, but rather we engage in theology as a radical stirring of voices that disturbs, provokes, analyzes, and transforms us. Intersectional theology alters the monolithic understanding of theology characteristic of traditional theologies and now views theology as a dynamic spoke with experiences, concepts, issues, identities, and ideas that all intersect, interconnect, and interrelate with each other. To recognize that there are multiplicities of genders and sexualities, and that this intersects with class, ethnicity, and race forces us to recognize that we cannot remain the same when we do theological reflection or discourse. The intersections of these important strands of identity affect how we understand God, humanity, sin, church—each and every theological category.

This dynamic and radical reform of theology is not a fad that will pass but rather is a rethinking and reimagining that will transform the way we view and do theology presently and in the future. We cannot ignore the call of intersectionality but need to embrace its challenges, demands, and claims. This will move theology in future directions that recognize the contributions of multiple voices, viewpoints, and perspectives to our limited understandings of God. Rather than simply reinforcing and reifying existing metaphors and understandings, our intersectional theology should push at the margins, challenge theological norms, and invite radical reformation of our thinking.

QUESTIONS

1. How does the notion of a "theology of interdeterminacy" expand the ways you think about the process and content of theology? What does it mean for you to imagine holding multiple and competing experiences and understandings in mind at the same time? What does it mean for you to take seriously diverse ways of being and knowing?

2. Intersectional theology claims a bias toward justice. What biases do you see in other theologies? How might a bias toward justice affect how you do theology?

3. What challenges do feminist, womanist, mujerista, *minjung*, postcolonial, queer, and other liberation theologies offer to traditional theologies? How does intersectional theology challenge all of these theologies to avoid slippages?

4. What challenges/issues/affirmations arise when you ask this chapter's questions of your own theology?

5. Is intersectional theology a helpful way for you to reflect theologically about your own life and life experiences? Is intersectional theology a liberating way to do theology?

6. Can intersectional theology be seen as a form of resistance (resistance to patriarchy, racism, colonialism, gender binary, etc.)?

7. How can we move away from single-axis thinking and also move toward a both/and thinking?

8. How does intersectional theology challenge the center and the status quo? How can we work to shift the center? How can we learn to listen to other voices besides our own communities' voices?

4.

Applying Intersectionality to Theology and the Bible

What happens when we apply intersectionality to theological questions and biblical texts? In this section, we posit a few possibilities for ways intersectional thinking might expand our theologies and enhance our understandings of God, as well as complicate our readings of the biblical text and its applications to the contemporary life of faith.

Vivian May, drawing from the work of Maria Lugones, argues that intersectionality encompasses a cognitive shift toward multiplicity. This shift allows us to hold simultaneously divergent viewpoints and to be "more than one self, at once."[1] May explains that in this multiple framework, Lugones "exceeds the binary and is both, sometimes simultaneously, though this claim can seem implausible according to notions of a singular, coherent self in a singular (or monological) world."[2] She argues that this ability to be more than one self and retain contradictions is not brokenness or fragmentation; rather, it is a welcome plurality and ambiguity that holds to the logic of the multiple.[3]

What happens when we apply this framework to God? Traditionally theological discussions about God have left no room for ambiguity or plurality. Rather, theologians and philosophers have argued about the perfection of God, and this notion of God's perfection dominates the classical understanding of God as expressed in Platonic dialogues such as *The Republic*. To be perfect is to be unchanging and self-sufficient and

---

1. Vivian May, *Pursuing Intersectionality, Unsettling Dominant Imaginaries* (New York: Routledge, 2015), 44.
2. May, *Pursuing Intersectionality*, 45.
3. May, *Pursuing Intersectionality*, 45.

thus absent of plurality or ambiguity. A perfect being, then, cannot be affected or changed by anything outside itself.[4] Thus it cannot move, and therefore God, as perfection, cannot be moved.

Traditional thinking understands perfection in very static terms, and so, if God is perfect, then change in any direction is an impossibility because change would be either a move away from perfection or toward perfection. When something is perfect, there is no need to move or change. Aristotle believed that "the divine has nothing better than itself by which it may be changed."[5] This understanding passed into Christian theology at an early stage, and we find it in Philo, a Hellenistic Jew, in his treatise *Quod Deus sit immutabilis* (That God is unchangeable). Philo defends the impassibility of God and explains that any biblical passages that seem to speak of God suffering are to be treated as metaphors. To allow for God's suffering and change is to deny divine perfection.[6] From here, the concept of God as unchanging has permeated much of our Christian framework of who God is and dissuaded us from any notions of ambiguity within the being of God.

Descartes offers a psychological argument for God, reasoning that the very presence of the idea of God as a perfect being is proof of the actual existence of this perfect being. He argues that since our mind perceives that it is not perfect itself, it could not have fabricated the idea of a perfect being.[7] The material world is conceived of in a mechanistic fashion, and, even though God is needed to create the universe and sustain it, God is basically absent in the world.[8] Even for Anselm, God is the being who is so perfect that nothing more perfect can even be conceived.

Furthermore, Korean American theologian Jung Young Lee writes that a God whose nature is perfect and self-sufficient does not suffer. If God is love, God cannot be in God's own nature indifferent to the afflictions of God's children, and thus this identity of God with us is understood as the sympathy of God.[9] The divine is regarded as the perfection of the good[10] and is self-sufficient so that God cannot be affected by any human emotion. God is the final good and is immovable.[11] Hence much

---

4. Alister McGrath, *Christian Theology: An Introduction* (Oxford: Blackwell, 1994), 214.

5. Simplicius, *In Cael*, 289. Aristotle, *On Philosophy*, frag. 16, OT as cited by Monte Ransome Johnson, *Aristotle on Teleology* (Oxford: Oxford University Press, 2005), 72.

6. McGrath, *Christian Theology*, 214.

7. Edgar V. McKnight, *Jesus Christ in History and Scripture: A Poetic and Sectarian Perspective* (Macon, GA: Mercer University Press, 1999), 97.

8. McKnight, *Jesus Christ in History and Scripture*, 97.

9. Jung Young Lee, *God Suffers for Us: A Systematic Inquiry into a Concept of Divine Passibility* (Dordrecht: Martinus Nijhoff, 1974), 10.

10. Lee, *God Suffers for Us*, 28.

11. Lee, *God Suffers for Us*, 30, 31.

of our male-dominated theology has reinforced a God who is unmovable and unambiguous. Through the lens of intersectional theology, we recognize that this concept of God has not always been helpful; it does not reflect the experience of many of the world's people and doesn't allow room for liberation, multiplicity, and ambiguity.

Modern theologians still often imagine God as a singular, coherent self, and much theologizing is aimed toward rightly describing this God-self without inherent contradictions or multiplicities. In Sunday school classes at church, we often teach children songs such as "Yesterday, Today, Forever Jesus Is the Same,"[12] which reinforces the singularity of God—that God never changes and has no contradictions. If, however, we apply the logics of intersectionality, we can think of God as multiple, divergent, and contradictory, encompassing the totality of diverse experience. In this way, God is both/and, more rich and complex and nuanced than our either/or theologies that posit a fixed and singular identity for God. Intersectional theology moves us beyond simple pluralism. Rather than understanding the Christian God, Allah, and Brahma side by side, for example, perhaps we can imagine God as YHWH and Allah and Brahma and all of those and none of those. Perhaps we can explore how the plurality of these aspects of divinity reside in God, even as God is an inherent multiplicity. Again, by making space for greater complexity in the being of God, we open possibilities for a God who is both/and, whose complexity is wide and deep enough to embrace us all.

Western European theology, which focused on the maleness of God, has embraced a singular God. The notion that multiplicities reside in God was quickly eliminated from the early church fathers' writing and work. In the Old and New Testaments, the feminine understanding of God is present and embraced. We see this in the psalmist writings of wisdom/*hokmah* who was with her people and provided for them. We read about *hokmah* in Proverbs, Song of Songs, and Ecclesiastes and in the Apocryphal writings such as the Book of Wisdom, Wisdom of Sirach, and Baruch. We see wisdom/Sophia scattered all over the New Testament writings; Jesus is conveyed as Sophia in 1 Corinthians 1:24, "Christ is the power of God and the wisdom of God."[13] The feminine understanding of God that was prevalent in early Christian thinking was soon eliminated, and *logos* Christology was quickly embraced.

12. "Yesterday, Today, Forever," by Albert B. Simpson (1890), which is based on Hebrews 13:8 and Matthew 28:20. The refrain is "Yesterday, today, forever, Jesus is the same, All may change, but Jesus never—glory to His name! Glory to His name! Glory to His name! All may change, but Jesus never—glory to His name!"

13. For more discussion on the wisdom or Sophia of God, see Grace Ji-Sun Kim, *The Grace of Sophia: A Korean North American Women's Christology* (Cleveland: Pilgrim, 2002).

Greco-Roman thought influenced the early church fathers, and, in this framework, dualism was entrenched in their thinking and theological inquiry. Within dualism, maleness is preferred over femaleness, and *logos* over Sophia. In dualistic thinking, there was no room for multiplicity or contradictions but only a male-dominated view of God.

Even in our present context, where there is so much religious dichotomy and strife between various faith traditions and groups, we need to challenge a monolithic understanding of God and approach interfaith relations through the lens of intersectional theology. This will allow room for contradictions and multiplicities to prevail in our understanding and approach to God. This will open space for dialogue and embracing of the other, which is so needed in a world torn apart by fear and unresolved religious tensions.

In many ways, this approach is compatible with a Trinitarian theology, but it is more than that. It makes room for all of God's identities across our differences and experiences and aims toward justice. One of the important contributions of process philosophy to theology is a destabilization of the self; rather than a fixed identity that endures through time, process philosophy understands the self as a series of selves coming into and out of being. Intersectional theology destabilizes traditional theology's singular self of God, creating disruptions and fissures in which other and multiple selves find expression. This is not polytheism, however. Rather, this approach recognizes that the self, including God's self, is always multiple, both/and, and destabilized so that possibilities for newness, diversity, and authenticity of difference can exist in simultaneity without reverting to a single axis, a single experience, or a single self.

The application of intersectionality also means, importantly, that God is biased toward justice, as liberation theologies argue. What intersectionality adds to that understanding is that God's bias toward justice encompasses all of the differences/oppressions simultaneously. Intersectional thinking reminds us not to return to single-axis analysis to imagine God's bias toward justice but to continue to plumb the complexities of intersections of difference in oppression and liberation. Therefore, we cannot reduce feminist theology to gender; it must encompass race/ethnicity, social class, sexuality, and ability. Queer theology cannot simply explore sexuality; it must examine gender, race/ethnicity, and other forms of difference as they intersect in queer experience and interpretation.

Pneumatology has been one of the most neglected doctrines within theological exploration. The Spirit has been variously understood as feminine, masculine, or even neutered. The church cannot seem to decide how to approach the Spirit, and hence the Spirit has been pushed aside as the church has decided to maintain its focus on Jesus Christ.

When the church has centered the Spirit, it has also seemed to monopolize the Spirit. This was achieved by putting the word "holy" in front of the Spirit. In this way, the church seemed to announce that only Christians can have the Spirit. But if we look at indigenous cultures and religions around the world, we see that the Spirit has always existed in these cultures. The Hebrew Testament and the Christian Testament portray Spirit as wind, energy, breath, and life-giving spirit. The Japanese have a term *ki*, which means energy. *Ki* is part of other Japanese words such as *reiki* and *aikido*, which use *ki* or energy for healing and movement. In India, energy and wind exist as *prana*, and in Hawaii, energy is understood as *ha*. When one greets in Hawaii, one says "Aloha," which means "meeting face to face (alo) of the breath of life (ha)."[14] Thus Spirit is not just exclusive to Christianity but is found and present around the world. This global understanding of the Spirit, which intersects religion, culture, and society, can be a valuable approach to move forward in doing intersectional theology.

As it did exist, it was clear that the Spirit was complex, and ambiguous. Even the Old Testament says, "I am who I am, I will be who I will be" (Exod 3:14). Acknowledging the mystery of God means we inevitably must leave room for ambiguity because we finite beings will never understand the infinite. The Spirit of God, which is understood as "wind" and "breath" in both the Old and New Testaments, conveys this very notion of ambiguity[15]—that the Spirit will move as the Spirit moves, and we cannot see the Spirit. A similar understanding is also present in various indigenous cultures and religions around the world. Recognizing similarities found in different cultures should help us recognize that theology cannot remain pristine or pure but rather requires hybridity and mixing of ideas and cultures to inform our thinking and theology. In this way, we come to recognize the intersectionality of pneumatologies presented around the globe. Rather than being fearful of this reality, Christian theologians' embrace of these intersectional understandings is long overdue.

An example of the Spirit being intersectional is in the work of intercultural pneumatology. Intercultural pneumatology does a comparative study of the Spirit as found in different religious cultures. One that stands

---

14. Grace Ji-Sun Kim, *Holy Spirit, Chi and the Other: A Model for Global and Intercultural Pneumatology* (New York: Palgrave Macmillan, 2011), 27.

15. For more discussion on global understanding of the Spirit, see Grace Ji-Sun Kim's *Holy Spirit, Chi and the Other*.

out is the work of Spirit-Chi pneumatology, which shows the similarity between the Asian concept of Chi and the Christian understanding of the Spirit. Even though these two religious cultures use two different terms for the understanding of the Spirit, these words—Spirit and Chi—are defined in the same way. Holy Spirit and Chi are both understood as wind, breath, energy, warmth, and life-giving Spirit. Spirit exists in our everyday religious, cultural, and social understanding in the West as well as in the East. The concept of Spirit intersects the cultural realm in Asian society as it is used in *reiki*, taekwondo, tai-chi, acupuncture, and everyday health. Similarly, we see this in Christian practices of prayer, laying on of hands, and healing. These two concepts, Chi and Spirit, intersect the everyday lives of ordinary people.

INTERSECTIONALITY AS A TOOL FOR BIBLICAL INTERPRETATION

As a source for theology, the Bible plays a key role in either reinforcing the status quo or prompting action toward liberation. Applying an intersectional lens to biblical interpretation, therefore, is essential for disrupting dominant readings of the text that reproduce social hierarchies and power and imagining liberating readings that spur action and reflection toward justice. Feminist, womanist, and other liberation interpreters have given us important ways of approaching the biblical text with an eye toward liberating possibilities. Our contribution is to encourage a thorough intersectional lens at the center of biblical interpretation that recognizes the significance of interlocking oppressions within the text and within uses of the text. Particularly, we encourage analysis that interrupts the flattening of liberatory readings to a single identity or axis of oppression and explores the complexities of these interlocking systems and identities within the text and within the reader's own social location/context.

For example, Musa Dube from Botswana works within a postcolonial African feminist framework that critiques the intersections of imperialism, colonial power, gender, and poverty. She seeks both to decolonize the mind and to decolonize the biblical text by uncovering its colonial or decolonial contexts, possibilities, and applications. She asks whether the biblical text encourages travel to the lands of others, specifically with the intent of taking resources for "God, gold, and glory." Dube also examines how Scripture uses gender and divine representations to create subordination and domination and how the church has also used these passages to subjugate entire peoples and continents.

Delores S. Williams attempts to read and approach Scripture from the less dominant side or the underside of history. For example, Williams reexamines the story of Hagar and Sarah from the perspective and importance of the slave woman rather than from the traditional perspective from the viewpoint of Sarah. Williams believes that just as God helped Hagar, the slave woman, God will also help and be in the struggle of African American women who have also been enslaved in the United States. The multiple causes of African American women's suffering—racism, economic vulnerability, sexism—all intersect with one another to further oppress them as a group. African American women's context of poverty, surrogacy, violence, rape, and homelessness is something that must be addressed and made better, Williams argues. African American women believe that God is "involved not only in their survival struggle, but that God also supports their struggle for quality of life, which 'making a way' suggests."[16] God responds to Hagar's situation and helps her survive, and in the same manner God helps and responds to the needs of African American women.

Elisabeth Schüssler Fiorenza points out that even postcolonial readings of the New Testament are prone to reinscribe structures of domination by attempting to "rehabilitate" Christian writings rather than examine them self-critically.[17] She notes that feminist scholars have drawn attention to the continuing ways that rhetorics of domination—such as the use of imperial imagery and titles for God, as well as Paul's rhetoric of submission—maintain ideologies of domination even as they seek to offer anti-imperial interpretations.[18] In contrast, an intersectional reading will examine texts with not only an eye toward anti-imperial readings but also with specific attention to gender, race, class, and other forms of difference in order to achieve what Schüssler Fiorenza calls methods of "conscientization, detoxification, and decolonization."[19]

Intersectional readings of the Bible remind us of two important approaches to the text to be included in our historical-critical and liberatory interpretations. One approach requires awareness of how the interpreter's social location affects the reading; the other asks how intersectionality plays out in the biblical text itself.

Intersectionality recognizes that these forms of oppressive powers are all interrelated and therefore must be taken seriously to counter white

---

16. Delores S. Williams, *Sisters in the Wilderness: The Challenge of Womanist God-Talk* (Maryknoll, NY: Orbis, 2013), 22.
17. Elisabeth Schüssler Fiorenza, *The Power of the Word: Scripture and the Rhetoric of Empire* (Minneapolis: Fortress Press, 2007), 4.
18. Schüssler Fiorenza, *The Power of the Word*, 5.
19. Schüssler Fiorenza, *The Power of the Word*, 7.

supremacy, patriarchy, heteronormativity, and classism. This includes how one lives out faith that has been so deeply formulated by oppressive institutions.

Intersectional readings of the Bible begin with self-reflection to raise awareness of how our own social location as readers with intersecting identities informs, shapes, expands, or perhaps even obscures our readings of the text. Musa Dube begins her work on postcolonial feminist biblical criticism by sharing a story from sub-Saharan African oral tradition: "When the white man came to our country he had the Bible and we had the land. The white man said to us, 'let us pray.' After the prayer, the white man had the land and we had the Bible."[20] As she notes, the Bible was (and continues to be) a tool for facilitating imperialism. From their perspective as white European men, colonizers, including and especially missionaries, understood the Bible to support the colonization enterprise and its parallel Christianizing of African peoples. Dube says the story above "articulates the deep senses of betrayal for those of us who have endured the exploitation and humiliation of Western imperialism but still dared to call ourselves Christians."[21] For Dube, then, biblical readers must pay attention to the imperial contexts of the text, land, race, power, nation, and gender. "There is also an issue of gender," she writes, "which is visible by its absence."[22] Thus, for example, when Dube reads the biblical story of the hemorrhaging woman in Mark 5:24–43, she weaves together the biblical text, an oral African tale, and the story of "Mama Africa." From her perspective as an African woman, Dube interprets the biblical story as a story of the bleeding of Mama Africa under colonial powers. Dube explains that Mama Africa's "role exposes gender oppressions and other forms of oppression encountered by African women." Her method, she explains, draws from theories of social location and other theories that "hold that all readers interpret the text according to their social experiences and contexts."[23]

Queer readings of the biblical text offer particularly fruitful disruptions of traditional heteronormative interpretations, although a great deal of queer interpretation is done by white critics who overlook the intersections of their queerness—as a subordinate identity—with their whiteness or maleness or middle-class status—dominant identities. Truly inter-

---

20. Dube quotes this story from Takatso Mofokeng, "Black Christians, the Bible and Liberation," *Journal of Black Theology* 2 (1988): 23. Musa Dube, *Postcolonial Feminist Interpretation of the Bible* (St. Louis: Chalice, 2000), 3.

21. Dube, *Postcolonial Feminist Interpretation*, 6–7.

22. Dube, *Postcolonial Feminist Interpretation*, 20.

23. Musa Dube, "Fifty Years of Bleeding: A Storytelling Feminist Reading of Mark 5:24–43," in *Other Ways of Reading: African Women and the Bible*, ed. Musa Dube (Atlanta: Society of Biblical Literature, 2001), 50–60.

sectional readings ask us to bring both our subordinate and dominant identities to the reading of the text so that we are aware of how the invisibility of our privileged assumptions may keep us unaware of the workings of race or gender or social class in our readings, even as we queer the text. Nonetheless, queer readings often begin by acknowledging that the Bible has been a "text of terror"[24] for queer people. Nancy Wilson argues, then, that queer readings must offer more than a silencing of the texts of terror by identifying texts that affirm same-sex love and reconstructing queer identities of characters in the Bible, or what she calls "outing the Bible."[25] Complicating this understanding of texts of terror from her perspective as a womanist, Pamela Lightsey adds, "Black lesbians must contend with experiences and training that tells them not only that God is made in the image of their oppressor but that God hates them categorically."[26] Robert Goss and Mona West explain that queer readers must "struggle against heterocentric privilege that erases us from the text."[27] Queer interpretation, they note, articulates "the community's lived experience in and beyond the closet as well as in its particular concerns when encountering and appropriating the biblical text. . . . It is a strategy that takes into account the multifaceted nature of our community as gay men, lesbians, transsexuals[28] and bisexuals from different ethnicities, socioeconomic standings, and religious communities."[29]

In addition to examining the reader's own social location, intersectional readings look for intersections at work in the text itself and in the history of interpretation and application of the text. Reading Jesus as a Jewish man of the working class living under imperial power brings a depth of complexity to the biblical narrative of his life that moves us beyond the "stained-glass," mono-focal Jesus of much of traditional biblical interpretation. Furthermore, queering Jesus brings questions of sexuality and sensuality to the forefront of our reading of the text. Likewise, our feminist readings of the biblical text must bring an intersectional lens to our examinations of gender in the text.

Take for example, the story of Ruth and Naomi. As one of the few

24. Phyllis Trible, *Texts of Terror: Literary-Feminist Readings of Biblical Narratives* (Minneapolis: Fortress Press, 1984).
25. Nancy Wilson, *Our Tribe: Queer Folks, God, Jesus, and the Bible* (San Francisco: HarperCollins, 1995).
26. Pamela Lightsey, *Our Lives Matter: A Womanist Queer Theology* (Eugene, OR: Pickwick, 2015).
27. Robert Goss and Mona West, introduction to *Take Back the Word* (Cleveland: Pilgrim, 2000), 6.
28. This volume was published in 2000 before the word "transgender" became the preferred term. We would also include gender nonbinary, gender nonconforming, and gender-fluid persons as intended by this passage.
29. Goss and West, introduction to *Take Back the Word*, 4.

named women in the Bible who is the central character in her story, Ruth is of special interest to feminists. Kwok Pui-lan notes that Ruth has captured the attention of postcolonial feminist readers because she illustrates "the intersections among gender, class, race, ethnicity, and sexuality in cultural contacts and border crossings."[30] Ruth is an immigrant, a foreign woman, a Moabite. She is poor. She is widowed. She obeys her mother-in-law Naomi as a way to continue the line of her husband's "house" in Israel. So as not to be perceived as a threat, she must give up her own national and ethnic identity in order to be absorbed into the culture around her. And so Ruth does not challenge the dominant cultural and religious norms. When foreign women do challenge the cultural norm, they are understood as deviant and a threat to the power structure.[31] Thus for Ruth's survival, she forsakes her cultural heritage and identity and assimilates into Israelite society and marries Boaz and bears him a son, Obed (Ruth 4:13–17). Sarojini Nadar focuses on Ruth's identity as a widow in light of experiences of Hindu widows.[32] Queer readers also point to the centrality of the deep love between two women in this story. Celena Duncan notes that "she had found a path she could not quit, a path that stirred her to make a vow. Her love for Naomi superseded her procreative responsibilities. She did not choose to follow Naomi to shock or to be different. She was drawn by her heart and could only choose in favor of what would provide her the greatest emotional and spiritual health and well-being. Not even family ties could hold her or draw her back when measured against the forward pull of her love for Naomi."[33] As an Asian woman reading Ruth, however, Kwok emphasizes the likely power differential between mother-in-law and daughter-in-law and reminds readers not to overlook these significant factors rising from race/ethnicity and culture.[34]

The Samaritan woman at the well provides another clear example of the importance of intersectionality to exploring the biblical text. In John 4, Jesus encounters a Samaritan woman at a well. Samaritans were of mixed ethnicity. When most Jews were removed during the Babylonian exile, those left behind in Judah intermarried with local people. These

30. Kwok Pui-lan, *Postcolonial Imagination and Postcolonial Theology* (Louisville: Westminster John Knox, 2005), 101.
31. Grace Ji-Sun Kim, *Embracing the Other: The Transformative Spirit of Love* (Grand Rapids: Eerdmans, 2015), 94.
32. Sarojini Nadar, "A South African Indian Womanist Reading of the Character of Ruth," in *Other Ways of Reading: African Women and the Bible*, ed. Musa Dube (Atlanta: Society of Biblical Literature, 2001), 159–75.
33. Celena Duncan, "The Book of Ruth: On Boundaries, Love, and Truth," in *Take Back the Word*, ed. Robert Goss and Mona West (Cleveland: Pilgrim, 2000), 95.
34. Kwok, *Postcolonial Imagination*, 111.

Samaritans adopted local customs and religious practices, although they still worshiped the God of Israel. They accepted the validity of worship outside Jerusalem, and they had their own Aramaic version of the Pentateuch. Jews considered Samaritans as foreigners and did not engage with them. Furthermore, for a man to be engaged in conversation with a woman—especially a woman who had had five husbands—was very unusual in Jesus's time. Nonetheless, Jesus reaches out across differences of gender, ethnicity, religion, sexuality, and class to welcome this woman in a theological conversation. This woman exists at the margins of social power, at the center of these intersections, and yet her story demonstrates her confidence and intelligence as she engages Jesus in banter about religious matters.

Finally, Marianne Bjelland Kartzow offers an intersectional reading of Galatians 3:28 and the Colossian household codes. She notes, "Although the genre, dating, and authorship of these texts differ, their ways of structuring relationships follow a similar pattern, and both are used in present-day discussions about hierarchy and equality."[35] Noting the various intersecting identities of persons in the household codes—ranging from ruling and loving husbands, slaveholders, and parents to obedient wives, slaveholders, and parents to freeborn children obedient to parents and obedient slaves, male child slaves, and female child slaves—she argues, "When Gal. 3:28 is read to illuminate Col. 3:18-4:1, it seems insufficient to use gender as the only analytical category. The different ways these two texts talk about men and women can only be understood by emphasizing how gender intersects with the status of free and slave. Since these texts are involved in different gender discourses, Gal. 3:28 cannot easily function to counter or delegitimize the power structure of the household codes, as has been common in biblical scholarship."[36]

Intersectionality becomes an important tool for biblical interpretation, as it helps us unpack the context, culture, and the "behind the scenes" to get a deeper understanding of the multiple layers of identities and issues that add to the layers of oppression within the Bible and the cultures that read it. Traditional historical criticism can only take us so far in our quest to read the Bible in our own time and contexts. In particular, historical criticism is limited (though necessary) in its usefulness for reading with a bias toward justice.

We recognize that Scripture has been misused as a tool to engage in war, slavery, genocide, patriarchy, racism, homophobia, and colonization. Recognizing these histories of reading and employing Scripture

---

35. Marianne Bjelland Kartzow, "'Asking the Other Question': An Intersectional Approach to Galatians 3:28 and the Colossian Household Codes," *Biblical Interpretation* 18 (2010): 375.

36. Kartzow, "'Asking the Other Question,'" 387.

to maintain power and dominance, we recognize the urgent need to read Scripture through the lens of intersectionality. We need more and diverse people around the table to help interpret and understand this ancient biblical text and make it applicable to our lives today. We need people whose lives encompass the scope of race, ethnicity, gender, sexuality, ability, and class to help us make sense of a text that is embedded in patriarchy, colonialism, ancient Mediterranean culture, and Greco-Roman philosophy. The more people from intersecting lives and identities that can come to the table to help understand the biblical text, the greater the depth and complexity of our understanding and the broader the application of our interpretations in our work toward justice.

Theological method has been entrenched in white male European culture and philosophy. This theological method has only furthered the oppression of women, people of color, and people of different sexual identities. White male euro-theology has maintained the status quo and kept others in subordinate and subjugated positions. We must embrace intersectionality as a theological method to create new ways of understanding theology that will not only liberate the subordinated but will also liberate the dominant, the colonizer, the privileged as all join together to seek to build an equitable and just world that values and affirms all people across differences of race, ethnicity, gender, sexual identity, national origin, ability, age, religion, or socioeconomic class.

The next chapter will explore how we engage in practicing intersectional theology as an applied theology in the church. It will involve relinquishing one's privilege and working toward dismantling systems of oppression, particularly those at work in the church itself. Engaging in this work may be painful for some, but naming systems of oppression as sin and moving toward an intersectional church is necessary as we endeavor to be God's justice-seeking people.

QUESTIONS

1. What might it mean to you to think of God as multiplicity rather than singularity?
2. What does intercultural thinking add to ways of doing theology as an intersectional process?
3. How does your social location affect the way you read the Bible?
4. Choose a favorite biblical passage. What might an intersectional reading add to your understanding of the passage? How can you apply this passage to your own life or justice work?
5. How can we live out intersectional theology and biblical interpretations?
6. Is the concept of Sophia helpful in how you approach Christology? What about the Asian concept of Chi in understanding pneumatology?

5.

Practicing Intersectional Theology

This section calls on readers to imagine what it would look like for individual Christians and the church as a whole to center intersectionality in their/its practices. As a liberatory practice, intersectional theology means Christians must relinquish their individual privilege and work toward the dismantling of systems of oppression. Christians can no longer ignore racism, sexism, heterosexism, classism, ableism, and ageism. We need to name these interlocking systems of oppressions as sin and move toward reimagining a community that can live out intersectional theology. This section will explore possible applications of intersectional theology in the lives of individual Christians and the lives of faith communities and the church as a whole. In particular, we will examine what an intersectional theology might mean for the church's internal functions—membership, baptism, communion—and also the church's work in the world, particularly in our current political climate that has targeted already-marginalized people, often in the name of God.

INTERSECTIONALITY AND THE INDIVIDUAL CHRISTIAN

Intersectional theology calls us as individual Christians to examine our own commitments to justice and the extent of our actual embrace of differences within our practice of faith in daily life. In particular, intersectional thinking helps us understand identities as "a collective political subjectivity and conscious coalition that also leaves room for individual identity."[1] In other words, intersectionality is a critical back-and-forth between individual persons and the collective political identities in

---

1. Patricia Hill Collins and Sirma Bilge, *Intersectionality* (Malden, MA: Blackwell, 2016), 129.

which people find themselves within systems of domination and subordination. One's identity is not monolithic but rather multidimensional, complex, and intersectional, situated within interlocking structures of power. One's identity includes and is not limited to ethnicity, class, race, sexuality, gender, and ability, which all intersect and are interdependent. Our lives are complex and our multiple identities are not mutually exclusive. Therefore the axes of classism, racism, homophobia, ableism, and other issues play a role in characterizing ourselves and how we engage in the struggle for social justice. Audre Lorde states, "There is no such thing as a single-issue struggle, because we do not live single-issue lives."[2] As women of color, we don't just struggle with racism, we fight sexism, classism, and transphobia. As lesbians, we don't just fight homophobia, but also sexism, racism, classism, and ableism. We are multiple identities and we fight multiple issues as these issues intersect and are interrelated within systems of power and privilege.

An Asian American community is not a single group with one history and identity but is rather a diverse, multiple, nonconforming group, just as are the individual members of it. Similarly, the LGBTQ community is complex, with multiple identities and axes that overlap, interrupt, and intersect to make the community diverse and come alive and be vibrant. Such are the realities of the individuals who are part of these groups that society likes to lump together and try to make it homogeneous for simplicity. The oppressions that individuals experience are compounded and multiplied due to the interweaving and untangling of the multiple sites of identity.

Patricia Hill Collins and Sirma Bilge emphasize that this understanding of identity is then a starting point and not an end in itself. Rather, individual and group identities become the impetus for intersectional inquiry and praxis[3]—understanding our social location and the location of others across multiple categories of identity within a political context leads to reflection and action for justice in the world. Rather than seeing this sense of identity and social location as divisive and isolating, Collins and Bilge see it as an opportunity for creating coalitional space.[4]

Kimberlé Crenshaw argues that intersectional identities provide opportunities for coalitions as individuals identify places to work within and across groups. So, for example, she explains that the intersectional experiences of women of color mean that rather than simply organizing on the basis of race, women and men of color can also organize as a

---

2. Audre Lorde, "Learning from the 60s," in *Sister Outsider: Essays & Speeches by Audre Lorde* (Berkeley, CA: Crossing Press, 2007), 138.
3. Lorde, "Learning from the 60s," 132.
4. Lorde, "Learning from the 60s," 133.

coalition with race as a basis for coalition. In so doing, a group forms around issues of race but with attention to the power differences of gender.[5]

As individual Christians develop intersectional awareness, they can express greater attentiveness to working with others across differences and attending to power differences within groups. So, for example, we can imagine coalitions of straight and LGBTQ Christians working together for equality for LGBTQ Christians within the church, while working in coalition with non-Christian LGBTQ people for equality within society. Within these coalitions, intersectional praxis also demands attention to power differences across gender and gender identity, across race, across ability, across age, and across social class. Attention to our own intersectional identities increases our ability to make connections with those who share some facet of identity and to recognize the ways power works across our differences in identity. So, for example, white women and women of color may organize by gender to advocate for equity in church leadership, but they must attend to differences across race so that the impacts of race on women of color are not obscured and so white women do not replicate the exercise of power over women of color based on race. Similarly, Kelly Brown Douglas and Pamela R. Lightsey offer groundbreaking calls for womanist theologians to ensure that their organizing around the intersection of gender and race does not ignore homophobia in the black community and perpetuate discrimination against LGBTQ people.[6]

To live out our faith and spiritual journeys, we cannot bring just parts of ourselves, but we need to bring our whole selves. Our entire beings include the intersecting parts of our identity and our location within structures of power. Therefore, we must embrace, welcome, and accept our entire identities (and not simply the aspects that confer dominance) whether it be our nonconforming gender identity or queer sexual identity, which some communities of faith do not welcome, or our marginalized identity as persons of color who experience everyday harassment due to the color of our skin. Our individual relationship with God requires our whole beings to come to God so that we can live faithfully in God. This will help us to authentically live out the gospel message and work toward justice.

Our personal spiritual practices include prayer, meditation, reading

---

5. Kimberlé Crenshaw, "Mapping the Margins: Intersectionality, Identity Politics, and Violence against Women of Color," *Stanford Law Review* 43, no. 6 (July 1991): 1299.

6. Kelly Brown Douglas, *Sexuality and the Black Church* (Maryknoll, NY: Orbis, 1999), and Pamela R. Lightsey, *Our Lives Matter: A Womanist Queer Theology* (Eugene, OR: Pickwick, 2015).

the Bible, listening to the voice of God, and reflecting theologically upon our lives. These spiritual practices need to be lived out from the fluidity of our complicated identities. For example, how we approach and read Scripture arises out of our personal identity as a heterosexual Asian woman, or as a middle-class white lesbian, or as a poor Latina trans woman. These intersecting identities help us to read and interpret Scripture in a way that is liberating for all people. If our interpretation of Scripture continues to reinforce slavery, racism, homophobia, classism, marginalization, and patriarchy, then we are reading it all wrong. The central message of Jesus is to love everyone and to liberate those who are oppressed.

Jesus healed lepers. Lepers were the outcasts of society. Nobody wanted lepers around and thus they were placed on the outskirts of society. Even as they were thrown aside by society, Jesus loved them and healed them (Luke 17:11–17). When no one wanted to associate with lepers, Jesus welcomed them. This is the good news for us living intersectional lives. As spiritual individuals, we want to present our whole selves to Jesus, who accepts all of our intersectional identities.

As we pray and meditate, our experiences of oppression and domination play a role in how we pray and what we pray for. Intersectionality allows us to see the pain in the world and how we all need to be instruments in bringing love and peace rather than hatred and war. As Martin Luther King Jr. once stated, "True peace is not merely the absence of tension; it is the presence of justice."[7] Intersectional spirituality moves us into spaces of courageous meditation to find the strength and motivation to fight for justice for ourselves and for others who are systematically oppressed.

As part of our spiritual practice we try to hear the voice of God in the church on Sunday mornings and also every day of our lives. Intersectionality's focus on both/and rather than either/or encourages us to hear the voice of God in unconventional and unfamiliar places. We hear the voice of God crying out in the wilderness and in the pain when we see our brothers and sisters struggling under white supremacy, heteropatriarchy, Islamophobia, and other forms of oppression. We hear the small voice of God asking us to repent of our sins and move toward restoration and love. We are encouraged by the small voice of God to work against systems of oppression and toward communities of liberation, love, and joy.

Individual Christians attentive to intersectionality are aware of the

---

7. Martin Luther King Jr., *Stride Toward Freedom: The Montgomery Story* (New York: Harper & Brothers, 1958), 217.

simultaneous disadvantages and privileges at work in their own lives. They recognize the ways they are variously situated in relation to power and privilege, disadvantage and discrimination, and the ways their social location has impact on their lives, their theologies, and their embodiment of Christian faith. They approach relationships with others conscious of how these intersections shape interactions, and they pay special attention to how their own privileges may prevent them from comprehending the struggles and complexities of the lives of others who are differently situated. They bracket their own deeply held and cherished beliefs in order to make space for different, even competing, beliefs of others, in order to learn from others and engage in authentic dialogue that moves everyone toward greater justice and love. They use their privilege to work for social change, and they build alliances and coalitions across differences to work toward the beloved community. They refuse the divisions of the current political situation and see identities and identity politics as ways to make the workings of power across difference visible, to affirm those who are marginalized, and to identify strategies for positive change that benefit all humans. They see commitment to intersectional thinking as a tool to help them embody the gospel's call to love our neighbors, to love our enemies, and to do good to all. Intersectionality becomes a practice that attunes us to our neighbors' needs and helps us see our neighbors, even those who differ most from us, as full human beings, beloved of God, and our siblings in God's family.

INTERSECTIONAL COMMUNITY

Community is important for all people. In contrast to Western emphasis on individualism, some cultures value community far more than individuality. For example, in Asia, the community's needs and wishes are more important than those of individuals. That makes the wishes of the community take precedence over personal desires. The Korean language reflects the valuing of community over individuality. In Korean, one uses the plural possessive pronouns rather than the singular possessive pronouns even when one is talking about a singular possession. For example, one says, "our mom" rather than "my mom" even though that person is the only child. Another example is "our husband" rather than "my husband" even though the speaker is the only spouse. Hence Korean emphasizes the collective community as more important than the individual self. In Africa, the word *ubuntu* means "I am who I am because of who we all are." Linguistically, this demonstrates the importance of the community, particularly in its role in forming the individual.

The emphasis on community in many non-Western cultures provides a challenge to the West to move beyond its devotion to individuality to encompass a broader commitment to community.

Communities happen in many places. There are faith communities, neighborhood communities, sports communities, and many others. These communities exist and function to promote the desires of those who adhere to the community. Recognizing the importance of intersectionality in community can then move us toward a more welcoming community as we pay attention to differences and work toward justice for all people.

Intersectionality's both/and or same/different thinking is especially valuable in building and sustaining community as it challenges singular thinking that is exclusive and embraces thinking that is multiple and inclusive. In other words, intersectionality opens the boundaries of communities and welcomes diverse people and perspectives. Additionally, intersectionality means communities do not deny or ignore differences, fissures, and disagreements. Sometimes being in community means being in opposition if positions or behaviors harm or marginalize or erase. So a community may be at once both/and, unified and fractured, and yet still a community that is intentional in its work against oppression and toward justice. Since intersectionality refuses marginalization or erasure, it is also useful in community to identify those places where people suffer at the intersections, where people are unaware of privilege, and where power works to maintain systems of domination. Communities' commitment to life together means engaging in this work, even when it's difficult to be both/and. As Vivian May explains, "The both/and lens, though a less tidy, more difficult place to begin (and end), offers a way to evaluate a situation from multiple standpoints, creates room to identify shared logics while accounting for differences, and can be used to approach tensions or contradictions as having logics and implications of their own, rather than treating them primarily as problems to smooth over."[8]

THE INTERSECTIONAL CHURCH

As we think about the church as an intersectional community, we can imagine a reexamination of our practical theology. What is an intersectional church? What does intersectionality mean for our worship, our community, our leadership, our pastoral care, our engagement with jus-

---

8. Vivian May, *Pursuing Intersectionality, Unsettling Dominant Imaginaries* (New York: Routledge, 2015), 65.

tice movements? In many ways, the contemporary church seems to be failing at its most basic tasks. Once-dominant Christian denominations that were largely white are in decline. White Christians are now fewer than half of the American public: "only 43% of Americans identify as white and Christian, and only 30% as white and Protestant."[9] While mainline Protestant denominations have been in decline for some time, in the decade between 2006 and 2016, the proportion of white evangelical Protestants fell from 23 to 17 percent. The proportion of white Catholics dropped from 16 percent in 2006 to 11 percent in 2016.[10] White Christians are also aging. Only 11 percent of white evangelical Protestants, 11 percent of white Catholics, and 14 percent of white mainline Protestants are under thirty years old. Sixty-two percent of white evangelical Protestants, 62 percent of white Catholics, and 59 percent of white mainline Protestants are at least fifty years old. The youngest religious groups in the US are Muslims, Buddhists, and Hindus.[11] Twenty-four percent of Americans are religiously unaffiliated, a statistic that is highly stratified by age. Forty-six percent of LGBTQ Americans are religiously unaffiliated.[12] About a third of millennials are religiously unaffiliated, and they are likely to become even less religious as they age.[13]

In some ways, these trends point to the overall shifts in racial demographics in the US. Simply put, people of color are a larger percentage of the population, and so we would expect that they would become a larger proportion of the Christian population as well. But when we take into account the intersections of race with age, sexual identity, and religious affiliation, we see another trend, as the PRRI report documents: Americans are disaffiliating with religion. Why? Many of the reasons have to do with the church itself. At the top of the list in one study is the inability to reconcile faith and science. Young people choose science over the church's mandate to accept ideas that contradict sound science (such as evolution). Other reasons people leave include church sex-abuse scandals, church hierarchy, the church's treatment of LGBTQ people, and the harm done to people by organized religion.[14]

---

9. Daniel Cox and Robert P. Jones, "America's Changing Religious Identity," September 6, 2017, https://tinyurl.com/yd5lnt6e.
10. Cox and Jones, "America's Changing Religious Identity."
11. Cox and Jones, "America's Changing Religious Identity."
12. Cox and Jones, "America's Changing Religious Identity."
13. Daniel Burke, "Millennials Leaving Church in Droves, Study Finds," May 14, 2015, https://tinyurl.com/p6govx8. Pew Research Center, "U.S. Public Becoming Less Religious," November 3, 2015, https://tinyurl.com/pcyjbot.
14. Michael Lipka, "Why America's 'Nones' Left Religion Behind," August 24, 2016, https://tinyurl.com/h8eyhl3.

These trends suggest the church is not meeting the needs of many people and, without significant change, may find itself becoming more and more irrelevant. The church's own history is one of power and dominance that has subordinated entire groups of people and continues to influence today's church in ways that are often exclusive and harmful. Rarely has the church's examination of itself fully included an understanding of intersectionality and a reckoning with the ways power is deployed in the church against women, people of color, LGBTQ people, the poor, people with disabilities, and people in the Two-Thirds World. An intersectional church must take account of the church's history and its ongoing oppressive behavior in order to imagine a transformed institution that is fully inclusive, prophetic, and just.

The contemporary church cannot be understood apart from its history of colonialism, racism, misogyny, homophobia, and violence. An intersectional church must reckon with this oppressive past and its ongoing oppressive legacy in the contemporary church. This legacy is rooted in the intersections of race, gender, class, religion, and nation such that the dominant contemporary church is a product of the juncture of white supremacy, Western dominance, masculinity, heteronormativity, and economic and political power. The detrimental effects of the missionary enterprise and its partnership with Western colonialism continue in the modern Two-Thirds World. The legacies of slavery and segregation continue to keep people apart on Sunday morning as the church has simply embraced the separation of racially diverse people into ethnic congregations as standard practice. The church's long history of misogyny means that in many traditions churches still exclude women from ordained ministry; some churches exclude women from any leadership role that gives them influence or authority over men; in some churches women can't offer public prayer if men are present. Even some generally progressive denominations are still fighting over the inclusion of LGBTQ people in their churches. At the extreme, churches denounce LGBTQ people as sinful or disordered, unwelcome as they are without a commitment to renounce their sexuality. Other churches are more ambivalent. LGBTQ people may be members, but they may not hold leadership. They can attend church, but they can't be married there. Many churches have wed themselves to political powers and have abdicated moral authority in return for political pandering toward particular views about abortion, contraception, marriage, immigration, and even Confederate statues. Intersectionality, with its bias toward justice, demands that the intersectional church attend to this legacy and seek to revolutionize its welcome and embrace of God's people. All of these othered by the traditional, dominant church provide us with the starting point for an intersectional church that privileges their perspectives, honors their suffering, and welcomes them without exclusions, as Marcella Althaus-Reid contends.[15]

INTERCULTURAL COMMUNITY

Too often our churches have become "silos." By this, we mean that on Sunday morning, there is a church for the LGBTQ community, a church for Korean Americans, a church for African Americans, a church for the rich, and a church for the poor. People seem to like to worship together with people who are like them. Instead of intercultural ministry or intersectional communities of worship, we see communities that are silos made up of people who are mostly alike. On the whole, churches don't seem to attempt to welcome or integrate people into the larger intersectional community.

Often, even if churches manage to integrate diverse people into the community, they often expect these folks to adapt to the dominant culture of the church and its practices of worship, education, and ministry. Rather than taking seriously the implications of intersections of gender, race, ethnicity, sexuality, ability, nation, and social class, churches expect a conformity to dominant cultural practices, such as the type of music, the style of preaching, the practices of communion and prayer, and even the ways people dress or shout amen or raise their hands or don't. Maria Pilar Aquino argues that rather than seeking a single culture, churches should practice hybridity, blending multiple cultures and reflecting these diverse cultures in the practice of church.[16]

Hybridity recognizes that we are mixed. Robert Young reminds us that a hybrid is technically a cross between two different species and that therefore the term "hybridization" evokes both the botanical notion of inter-species grafting and the "vocabulary of the Victorian extreme right," which regarded different races as different species.[17] This concept of hybridization can be applied to our identities as human beings. We are mixed beings when it comes to ethnicity, race, culture, and identity. Hybridity reminds us that nothing is "pure," but everything and everyone is a mixture of two or more things.

15. Marcella Althaus-Reid, *Indecent Theology: Theological Perversions in Sex, Gender and Politics* (New York: Routledge, 2000), 4.
16. Maria Pilar Aquino, *Feminist Intercultural Theology: Latina Explorations for a Just World* (Maryknoll, NY: Orbis, 2007).
17. Robert Young, *Colonial Desire: Hybridity in Theory, Culture and Race* (London: Routledge, 1995), 145.

Postcolonial thinker Homi Bhabha reminds us why hybridity is a useful tool in doing intersectional theology. It is powerful: "The display of hybridity terrorizes authority with the ruse (trick) of recognition, its mimicry, its mockery."[18] Intersectional ministry will work to dismantle the status quo and challenge those in authority who hold power through its embrace of difference and multiplicity against sameness and singularity. This focus on difference, multiplicity, and hybridity can help the church challenge oppressive powers and imagine new ways of living equity and justice.

Applying intersectional thinking to the practices of the church can lead to truly intercultural communities and intercultural ministries. Intercultural churches and ministries move beyond diversity and question how ministries relate to others and how power structures exclude certain people and keep certain groups of people powerless and subordinate within the church. In many churches and ministries, "different cultures may exist side by side, but they do not come together to learn from one another and to engage one another in mutual relationships. They do nothing to change the power imbalances that persist when one culture remains dominant. They may be diverse but they are not intercultural."[19] Intercultural churches and ministries bring people of all cultures together to learn from one another and give equal value and power to all. Within these intentional intercultural communities, redistribution of power and transformation of practices are key to living out intersectionality.

Furthermore, intercultural churches and ministries are "defined by justice, mutuality, respect, equality, understanding, acceptance, freedom, peacemaking, and celebration"[20] and offer many transforming ideas and possibilities in living out an inclusive and just faith. African American theologian Dwight Hopkins reminds us that the "life of Jesus and the best of Christian legacies compel us to enter into a way of life of intercultural engagement—the interaction of people across races, ethnicities, and nationalities to learn to value and celebrate each group's traditions."[21]

Intersectionality adds to intercultural ministry's inclusiveness an attention to the ways power operates across difference and within groups. Intersectional theology compels us to go beyond race, ethnicity, and nationality and to be mindful of all the simultaneous various identities of individuals and communities that intersect and to call out the unjust

---

18. Homi Bhabha, *The Location of Culture* (London: Routledge, 1994), 115.

19. Grace Ji-Sun Kim and Jann Aldredge-Clanton, *Intercultural Ministry: Hope for a Changing World* (Valley Forge, PA: Judson, 2017), x.

20. Kim and Aldredge-Clanton, *Intercultural Ministry*, x.

21. Dwight Hopkins, "Foreword," in *Intercultural Ministry: Hope for a Changing World*, ed. Grace Ji-Sun Kim and Jann Aldredge-Clanton (Valley Forge, PA: Judson, 2017), v.

powers of oppression and subordination. Therefore, intersectional theology calls us to imagine a new church and new ministries that center multi-axis thinking in our quest to be the people of God in community together. Beyond simply welcoming people with all their different identities and backgrounds, intersectional theology calls us to transform church into a vibrant, inclusive, and ever-changing community at work for justice in the world. It challenges us to create new models of becoming church in which the various intersecting identities awaken us to new sensitivities and ways of becoming the body of Christ. An intersectional church will transform silos and shared buildings into truly intercultural communities that reflect the diverse constituent groups, differences within and across groups, and attention to the dynamics of power at work in structures and relationships.

Intersectional thinking, however, also reminds us that whenever there is community, we find those who are outside the community. As Natalie K. Watson writes, "A feminist theological critique points out that human beings are in fact different but that in the context of Christian theology and praxis that difference cannot be the basis for exclusion or marginalization but is rather a factor of enrichment for the church."[22] Intersectional thinking calls for us to be attentive to the possibilities for exclusion based on difference and to expand the boundaries of community toward greater inclusion of difference and multiplicity. An intersectional church must attend not only to difference with the church but also to those outside the church; we must also create just relationships and communities with people who participate in religions other than Christianity or no religion at all. Kwok Pui-lan points to the importance of questioning religious boundaries, particularly in light of Asian feminist theologians' embrace of syncretism as a way to disrupt rigid notions of religious identity.[23] She notes that "Christianity has never been pure and has continuously, from its beginning, adopted elements from different cultures. It is only when non-Western churches are doing so that more established churches and theologians label such practices as 'syncretism' in a derogatory sense, to exercise control and power."[24] The relation between gospel and culture, she argues, has always been one of negotiation and contestation.[25] She notes, particularly in Asia, interplay among Asian religions and Christianity has always allowed more fluidity than in Western prac-

---

22. Natalie K. Watson, *Introducing Feminist Ecclesiology* (Eugene, OR: Wipf & Stock, 1996), 49.
23. Kwok Pui-lan, *Postcolonial Imagination and Feminist Theology* (Louisville: Westminster John Knox, 2005), 145.
24. Kwok, *Postcolonial Imagination and Feminist Theology*, 161.
25. Kwok, *Postcolonial Imagination and Feminist Theology*, 161.

tices of Christian faith. She explains, "Such religious experience allows room for cultural hybridity and cross-fertilization between different traditions."[26] Elizabeth A. Johnson explains that God can be discovered in the encounter of religions. She writes, "At the outset it opens the possibility that others might have distinct encounters with the divine that can be new resources for Christian exploration into the overabundance of God. To put it simply, the living God is not a Christian. Rather, the incalculable mystery, which the Christian Scripture dares to call love (I John 4:8 and 16) is not constrained in loving but freely pours out affection to all and each one."[27]

INTERSECTIONAL ECCLESIOLOGY

Feminist ecclesiologies offer us a way forward in thinking about an intersectional church. Because of the church's history as a place for the exercise of white, male, heterosexual power, women, people of color, and LGBTQ people often have a fundamentally ambivalent attitude toward the church. As Natalie K. Watson points out in her introduction to feminist ecclesiology, the history of the church is both one of women's suffering and one of meaningful spaces in which women have developed their own discourses of faith.[28] In other words, the church has simultaneously been a place of oppression and empowerment for women. Similarly, the church both provided biblical and theological justification for slavery and segregation and offered a place for African Americans to create support and resistance. Yet, even within these frameworks of oppression and empowerment, intersections of difference have further complicated people's experiences. White Christian feminists have not always been attuned to the issues of women of color. Male leaders within the black church have often relegated women to subordinate status. Generally speaking, the church has and continues to scorn and debase LGBTQ people across gender, race, and nationality.

Intersectional awareness can help us move the ecclesiological conversation beyond liberation for groups based on single-axis thinking to a fully inclusive and complicated embrace of justice within and across groups. As Watson notes, the question of ecclesiology is not simply "What is the church?" It is also, "Who is the church?"

The question of "who?" reminds us of the human beings who make

---

26. Kwok, *Postcolonial Imagination and Feminist Theology*, 162.
27. Elizabeth A. Johnson, *Quest for the Living God: Mapping Frontiers in the Theology of God* (New York: Continuum, 2007), 162.
28. Watson, *Introducing Feminist Ecclesiology*, 2–3.

up the community and institution of the church. We all exist in complicated identities, contexts, and cultures within systems of power. As we live in various contexts, we recognize that our lives have many cultural, socioeconomic, racial, sexual, and gender intersections that deepen and enrich our lives and constrain and challenge us. These various forms of identities all collide, affect, and weave into each other within these structures of power, highlighting the multiple sites of identities, institutions, and resistance in which we can learn to be church and understand God. Watson points out the importance of the question of "who?" in imagining ecclesiology. She asks, "What does it mean for women to be part of the 'body of Christ' when their own bodies are rendered impure and excluded from the most significant moments in its life? . . . Can the church be relevant to lesbians and women who do not see heterosexual marriage as a key part of their identities if the relationship between Christ, the male head of the Church, and his bride, the submissive feminine Church, is perceived by some as the fundamental structure of all relationships?"[29] Delores S. Williams complicates these questions with attention to intersections to race and social class. Writing of liturgy, she asks, "How does this source portray blackness/darkness, women and economic justice for nonruling-class people?" She concludes, "A negative portrayal will demand omission of the source or its radical reformation by the black Church."[30]

Drawing from African women's social location, Mercy Amba Oduyoye envisions the church as "the hearth-hold of Christ within the household of God."[31] Challenging the notion of "household" as a metaphor for the church, Oduyoye draws on the work of Felicia I. Ekejiuba who argues "that the householder is not necessarily the focal point of well-being of [the African family]." Instead, she notes that African families are "organized around the hearths of women, some of whom may be biological mothers but not necessarily so."[32] Oduyoye goes on to point out that in African religions, "All human beings are the people of God," and, in God's household, "religious people discern many hearth-holds." She explains that this metaphor is in contrast to a "triumphant Christology" that assumes that Christ is the "monopoly of Christians."[33] She contrasts this vision of the church as "hearth-hold" with the actual experience of most women in finding that their "experience of the Church is no

---

29. Watson, *Introducing Feminist Ecclesiology*, 12.

30. Delores S. Williams, "Womanist Theology: Black Women's Voices," in *Feminist Theology from the Third World: A Reader*, ed. Ursula King (Eugene, OR: Wipf & Stock, 1994), 84.

31. Mercy Amba Oduyoye, *African Women's Theology* (Cleveland: Pilgrim, 2001), 79.

32. Oduyoye, *African Women's Theology*, 78.

33. Oduyoye, *African Women's Theology*, 79.

different from the culture outside the Church structures," and she warns that "often they experience more recognition of their humanity outside of the Church."[34] An intersectional understanding of church demands that we transform the church into a space of justice that recognizes, welcomes, and affirms full humanity across differences of gender, sexuality, race, economics, and nation. Oduyoye explains that "together" means "together as women and men, together as north and south, together as black and white."[35] She concludes, "The ecclesiological emphasis that women bring, is that which holds the Church accountable to being a community that lives the life of Christ, that preaches the reign and love of God by its being and doing, serves God's people and God's purposes and presents itself as a sample of *koinonia* approved of and by God, and in which God participates."[36]

An intersectional ecclesiology must account for all of God's people, inclusive of their differences and places within the matrix of domination. Drawing from the questions of intersectionality for theology generally, we can also ask these questions of our ecclesiology:

- How does my own social location (at the intersections of both dominant and subordinate identities) affect how I understand church?
- How is my understanding of church contextualized within the larger settings of nation, denomination, culture, era?
- What is the history of my interpretive community's understanding of church, and how does my interpretive community influence my understandings of church?
- Am I using single-axis thinking as I reflect on church or am I keeping multiple, intersecting, and sometimes competing perspectives and identities in mind as I imagine church?
- How am I ensuring that my thinking about church is both/and?
- How is power at work in these understandings of church? How do these ideas of church distribute power?
- Does this understanding of church reproduce or challenge inequities? Does it expose and restructure power relations?

---

34. Oduyoye, *African Women's Theology*, 81.
35. Oduyoye, *African Women's Theology*, 88.
36. Oduyoye, *African Women's Theology*, 89.

- How can my understanding of church be liberatory? How is it biased toward justice?
- How do I hold multiple and competing voices about the church in mind at the same time? Do I take seriously the realities of others without looking for an underlying sameness or attempting to universalize my own ideas about church? Have I bracketed various discourses about church and entered into the logics of realities not my own?
- Does my thinking about church destabilize fixed notions of church?
- Do my ideas about church act in collusion with dominant powers?
- Do my ideas have the potential for radical reforming of how we think about and practice church?

Theologies of liberation call our attention and demand our action toward justice. A first step is the church's recognition of its own role as an institution in the matrix of domination and its collusion with the social, economic, and political forces of domination and oppression. The church must redeem itself in relation to women, whom it has blamed for evil in the world and subjected to second-class status; to people of color and people in the Two-Thirds World, against whom the church has supported slavery, segregation, colonization, and genocide; to LGBTQ people, whom the church has excluded, persecuted, and belittled; to the poor, whom the church has ignored or victimized in favor of the wealthy; and to people with disabilities, whom the church has blamed for their differences or has marginalized in its theologizing.

The church must embrace the gospel's insistence on liberation and justice, embodied in the life and message of Jesus. We think about the story of the woman who anointed Jesus's feet (Luke 7:36–50). Jesus was having dinner with the Pharisees when a "sinful" woman came to the house with an alabaster jar of perfume. She wept and began to wet Jesus's feet with her tears, then wiped them with her hair, kissed them, and poured perfume on them. When the Pharisees saw this, they were upset. Jesus turned this scene around as a teaching moment of welcome for those we do not welcome. It becomes a powerful story for us, as it shows how to love those whom we find hard to love. It teaches us that we should not judge others because of their position, status, gender, or sexuality. Rather this story shows us how we need to work toward gender equality as Jesus accepts the "sinful" woman's anointing. Lynn Bell points out that the Gospels note the sexual histories of three women with whom Jesus interacts—although the Gospels ignore the sexual histories of the men Jesus encounters—the woman caught in adultery, the Samaritan woman who had had many husbands and was cohabitating with a man at the time of her meeting with Jesus, and the woman who anointed Jesus. Bell notes, "The Gospels not only make a point of reporting the women's sexual sins, but also of describing Jesus's response. First, he did not permit the Pharisees to harm the woman caught in adultery or to be cruel to the prostitute weeping at his feet. Second, Jesus himself did not scold, shame, or rebuke any of the three, even though according to Jewish law they had sinned. Nor did he appear to equate their sin with diminished human worth. He never labeled them according to their sexual misconduct. Even the actual prostitute was referred to by Luke with the more general euphemism, 'a woman who lived a sinful life.' And, though Simon the Pharisee shuddered at the sight of the prostitute touching Jesus, Jesus welcomed her kisses on his feet and commended her love and faith."[37]

The church's tendency to label entire groups of people "sinful" reinforces its exclusionary practices and expression of power over subordinated groups. For much of recent history, the church has labeled the entire LGBTQ community "sinful" because of their sexual and gender identities. In fact, most denominations and churches continue this practice, compounding the discrimination and oppression experienced by LGBTQ people every day in every place around the world. Yet the gospel's consistent message of welcome and inclusion challenges the church's historic practice of judgment and exclusion.

Gustavo Gutiérrez, who is considered the father of liberation theology, believes that theology is an understanding that must continue to grow and change. Theology cannot stay stagnant and cannot remain the same across history. Gutiérrez says that theology "linked to praxis, fulfills a prophetic function insofar as it interprets historical events with the intention of revealing and proclaiming their profound meaning."[38] Thus theology needs to change with the times. This does not mean that we forget the past, but rather we look at it with the intention of making a difference in our present life context. Harvey Cox agrees, writing that "the only future that theology has, one might say, is to become the theology of the future."[39]

Theology must be liberative and work toward justice. Gutiérrez

---

37. Lynn Bell, "She Is More Than," *Mutuality* 19, no. 1 (2012): 14.
38. Gustavo Gutiérrez, *A Theology of Liberation* (Maryknoll, NY: Orbis, 1990), 10.
39. Harvey Cox, *On Not Leaving It to the Snake* (New York: Macmillan, 1967), 12.

reminds us of our need for "a theology which is open—in the protest against trampled human dignity, in the struggle against the plunder of the vast majority of humankind, in liberating love, and in the building of a new, just and comradely society—to the gift of the Kingdom of God."[40] We need to stand up alongside those who are oppressed, particularly those oppressed by the church, and participate in the struggle to transform sinful structures of power that diminish anyone's full humanity. This is how church becomes the kin-dom of God.

We also must, however, be sure that in our zeal to address particular forms of oppression—sexism, racism, heterosexism, classism, ableism—we do not overlook the intersections and return to single-axis thinking. We only move the church toward real justice when we make room for differences, when we engage in both/and thinking, when we bracket competing discourses, and when we commit ourselves to justice with no exceptions. The question of intersectionality for ecclesiology provides a necessary framework for our theologizing about church, centers difference and multiplicity, accounts for structures of power, and ensures our trajectory toward justice.

THE RESISTANT CHURCH

On the whole, the church's history is primarily one of collusion with dominating powers. Of course, across this history are scattered examples of a counter-church, a church resisting the dominating powers of racism, misogyny, transphobia, ableism, capitalism, homophobia, xenophobia, colonialism, and ageism. Intersectionality calls the church to be the resistant church. With an awareness of intersecting identities and interlocking systems of oppression, the church must resist the organization of structures of power that maintain the dominance of the elite. Following the example of Jesus, the church must stand against worldly powers that force the poor and vulnerable and marginalized into ever-more constrained spaces, seeking their invisibility and, ultimately, their destruction. Read from an intersectional perspective, the gospel is a story of Jesus's resistance to the religious and political powers of his day in favor of the socially, economically, politically, and religiously oppressed. This resistance led to his crucifixion. But the story tells us that God rewarded Jesus's resistance, and the resurrection is the evidence of the truth of Jesus's cause. The intersectional church can do no less than follow Jesus in his commitment to radical welcome, inclusion, and transformation. Even as the church embraces all of God's children, as theologies of

---

40. Gutiérrez, *A Theology of Liberation*, 12.

liberation teach, the church, like God, must side with the oppressed. The church of intersectional theology is not the church triumphant, but the church resistant.

THE PRACTICE OF INTERSECTIONALITY

Delores S. Williams suggests that for womanist theology, methodology should be informed by four elements: "(1) a multidialogical intent, (2) a liturgical intent, (3) a didactic intent, and (4) a commitment both to reason *and* to the validity of female imagery and metaphorical language in the construction of theological statements."[41] Multidialogical activity allows dialogue and action across differences and toward justice. Liturgical intent ensures theological method is relevant to the black church in general and black women in the church in particular. Didactic intent expresses the church's teaching function, particularly in relation to justice. And, finally, theological language rooted in the experiences of black women can invigorate the life of the church and empower social and theological change. Drawing from Williams's suggestions, we can imagine an intersectional church engaged in dialogue and action across differences, ensuring the relevance of the church's worship and ministry to all people, teaching the theory and practice of justice with intersectionality at the center, and transforming itself and society with theological language and practice that encompass the totality of human experience and worth.

What, then, might a truly intersectional church look like? Certainly not the silos that now characterize Sunday mornings. Susan's church, Ainsworth United Church of Christ in Portland, Oregon, looks like an intersectional church, both in its membership and in many of its practices. In the 1980s, two separate UCC congregations, one predominantly black and one predominantly white, had churches in the same north Portland neighborhood. Leaders in both congregations, however, had a vision for a single church united by its commitment to multiracial justice, and so the congregations combined. From its beginning, the church was committed to gender as well as racial justice, calling women as pastors and engaging women in every level of church leadership. While the church always welcomed LGBTQ people, it participated in the formal process of becoming "open and affirming" in the 1990s. The church describes itself as "a multi-cultural, multi-racial, open & affirming, Just Peace and accessible church. We celebrate that God is still speaking in our world today and that God's extravagant welcome and love is for

---

41. Williams, "Womanist Theology," 83.

everyone."⁴² These words are also embodied in the church's membership—people of many races, nationalities, cultures, genders, sexualities, and economic backgrounds. Also, importantly, these words are embodied in the church's practices. Worship features music from black gospel tradition, the civil rights movement, and Spanish-language hymns as well as from classical tradition. The multilingual pastor offers greetings in many languages, which the congregation repeats. A painting of a black Madonna hangs on the wall of the sanctuary. Announcements highlight local social justice work opportunities, and the church participates regularly in Portland's interfaith community. The church's website explains, "Ainsworth is a justice-loving church. We believe we are called by our faith to love our neighbors and to seek equality, welcome, justice, and community for all. Our tradition calls us to put our faith in action, and to respond to injustice through action and reflection, through protest as well as prayer."⁴³

Middle Collegiate Church in New York City is another church that exemplifies intersectional theology. The senior minister is Rev. Dr. Jacqui Lewis who is an African American woman. The church is ethnically diverse and welcomes people from all walks of life. They've built a faith community that is oriented toward healing souls so they can heal the world. Middle Church works for racial justice, LGBTQ/gender equality, and economic justice. They have many programs for the community, including arts programs for children, twelve-step programs, and the Momentum Project, which offers free community lunch and food pantry once every week. They also hold an annual conference called "Revolutionary Love," which trains churches and individuals to use love-in-action to create a more just society.

The character of the early church comprised *kerygma*, *diakonia*, and *koinonia*. These three characteristics may be helpful to us today as we practice intersectionality in our churches. *Kerygma* is the good news that is preached in the church. The church is born and comes alive through the preaching of the gospel message. Without preaching there is no church.⁴⁴ To live out intersectionality in the everyday, the sermon or the *kerygma* preached needs to be intersectional. The good news that is shared must be the good news of God's love for *all people* and not a selective few. God's grace and mercy are for all and not just for dominant white heterosexual men.

---

42. Ainsworth United Church of Christ website, http://ainsworthucc.com.
43. Ainsworth United Church of Christ website, https://tinyurl.com/y8prvf27.
44. Joseph Pungar, *Theology Interpreted* (Lanham, MD: University Press of America, 1993), 127.

Power resides in preaching the good news that embraces all people. This is the good news that Jesus shared. Jesus proclaimed that "you shall love the Lord your God with all your heart, and with all your soul, and with all your mind, and with all your strength, and you shall love your neighbor as yourself. There is no commandment greater than these" (Mark 12:30–31). The second part of the commandment, which asks us to love our neighbor, is difficult to follow when we are unsettled by our neighbors' race, gender, sexuality, class, ability, or nation of origin as if something is wrong with our neighbor. Jesus placed no conditions on his commandment. We are to love all of our neighbors.

The good news that all are welcomed into the family of God is powerful and needs to be a lived reality. Our identities intersect and so should our ways of preaching the message of the sermon. Therefore as pastors and leaders of the church who preach and share the good news, we must interpret Scripture intersectionally and preach it as a necessary component to living out faithfully and justly the good news of the gospel.

The second characteristic is *diakonia*. *Diakonia* is about the church's social responsibility and the basis of charity. The early Christians could not accept that some of them lived in need and in poverty. So the rich people in the churches found a way to help the needy. They did this by selling their property and placing their funds at the disposal of the church. In this way, they created community and realized that this was the work of the Holy Spirit.[45] An intersectional theology demands the church fulfill its social responsibility to address poverty, class, wealth, and capitalism, along with the intersections of gender, race, sexuality, ability, age, and religion. These are the intersecting realities that continue to perpetuate the status quo and marginalize the poor in our society and in our churches.

We like to reference biblical passages such as "For you always have the poor with you, but you will not always have me" (Matt 26:11) as a way to relieve ourselves of the task of addressing poverty in our wider society. But a both/and intersectional reading of the text shows us that we can both minister to the needs of the individuals right in front of us and care about the larger systems that trap people in cycles of poverty and neglect. Yes, the poor are always with us, but that does not mean that we don't seek ways to make our society more just, more equitable so that we eradicate poverty. We can fight the rich 1 percent and create laws that are more just and make the rich pay their share of taxes and give back to society. Furthermore, the practice of intersectionality seeks out different avenues so that we can address the fact that it isn't a problem

---

45. Pungar, *Theology Interpreted*, 127.

of poverty, but rather a problem of wealth[46] that needs to be distributed more equally and justly.

When we practice intersectional ministry, we become aware that poverty, gender, and race are usually tied together. The poorer in American society are usually people of color, and generally more women are poor than men. The Institute for Research on Poverty reports that "the poverty rate among blacks is more than two times greater than the 11.4 percent poor rate for whites."[47] Pearce uses the term "feminization of poverty"[48] to identify the increasing poverty rate among women and their children. The church's ministry of social responsibility and eradicating poverty recognizes the intersectional aspect of its ministry, and, while addressing the needs of the specific poor people in front of us through projects and programs to provide food and housing, for example, it also works toward systemic transformation to end poverty completely.

Koinonia is the third characteristic of the early church. It is the community and fellowship of believers (Acts 2:42). This community includes all peoples and cannot be exclusive. Often the church, like most people in the time of Jesus, wants to exclude "lepers" as they are undesirable and carry "disease." Some churches have labeled certain groups like the LGBTQI community, people of color, the poor, immigrants, or women as "lepers" who should not be welcomed in the fellowship of believers.

I (Grace) spoke at The Reformation Project[49] conference in Chicago. The Reformation Project works for the full inclusion of the LGBTQ community. Around 450 people attended the conference, where I was one of the keynote speakers. At the conference, I met many people who shared stories of being rejected by the church. Either they or their family members were told to leave because of their sexuality. They shared how their churches preached not about inclusion but rather about exclusion. Their churches preached that homosexuality was a sin and that LGBTQ people are "bad people." The depth of pain experienced by these people reveals that *kerygma* needs to be preached and that *koinonia* needs to be practiced. Ministers must consider and give priority to intersectionality when sharing the good news. Otherwise, it is not the good news for everyone.

---

46. For more discussion on this issue, see Elizabeth Hinson-Hasty, *The Problem of Wealth: A Christian Response to a Culture of Affluence* (Maryknoll, NY: Orbis, 2017).
47. "Who Is Poor?," Institute for Research on Poverty, https://tinyurl.com/y8vjn5xt.
48. D. Pearce, "The Feminization of Poverty: Women, Work, and Welfare," in *Urban and Social Change Review* 11 (1978): 28–36.
49. See The Reformation Project website for more information: https://www.reformationproject.org.

If we are to move toward an intersectional way of doing ministry, we need to be mindful of the axes of intersectionality and be welcoming and embracing of all people as we gather for worship, prayer, and the sacraments.

BAPTISM AND COMMUNION

Feminist theologians call for a reformation of the church's practices in its sacraments, particularly baptism and communion, which are shared by almost all Christian denominations. Natalie K. Watson points to the problem of the construction of women in churches as merely recipients of the sacraments rather than full participants in them.[50] She asks, "If sacraments are enactment of Christ's presence at crucial stages in the course of life, then we have to ask whether the inherited sacramental canon of the church fits the crucial events in a woman's life or if it is based on the assumption of a church dominated by male human beings." She adds, "we cannot restrict ourselves to attributing some aspects of Christlikeness to men and others to women, such as attributing Christlike authority and leadership to men and Christlike submission, obedience, and servanthood to women."[51] For women, both baptism and communion have been experiences of exclusion as they have usually been denied the right to administer the sacraments and to receive the sacraments from women.

Certainly baptism and communion are meant to function as symbols of equality and inclusion. In baptism, all are fully and equally welcomed into the church, and, in communion, all are equally welcome at the table, although both rituals in most churches do reinforce boundaries of who is in and who is out of the community. Watson acknowledges that the equality of baptism is "still initiation into fundamental ambiguity." While all may be equal in baptism, that equality does not extend into the ecclesial communities where women and LGBTQ people do not experience full equality. Watson asks, "What does baptism communicate and does baptism indeed provide a challenge to the church which it needs to learn to live up to?"[52]

The church has debated for a long time about who can be baptized. The Donatist controversy was named after the breakaway African church leader Donatus. The Donatists were a group of native African Christians, based in modern-day Algeria, who resented the growing

---

50. Watson, *Introducing Feminist Ecclesiology*, 78.
51. Watson, *Introducing Feminist Ecclesiology*, 81–82.
52. Watson, *Introducing Feminist Ecclesiology*, 86.

influence of the Roman church in northern Africa. The Donatists argued that the church was a body of saints and not a place of sinners. The issue became important during the persecution undertaken by the emperor Diocletian in 303 and lasted until the conversion of Constantine in 313. During this persecution, in which possession of Scripture was illegal, a number of Christians handed in their copies of Scripture to the authorities and were condemned by others who refused to cave in under persecution. After the persecution died down, many of these *traditores* (literally "those who handed over their Scriptures") rejoined the church but the Donatists argued for their exclusion.[53]

The Donatists believed that if a bishop lapsed under persecution, the bishop had committed the sin of apostasy ("falling away"). As a result, he placed himself outside the bounds of the church and could no longer be regarded as administering the sacraments validly. The Catholics on the other hand argued that by the bishop's repentance, the bishop had been restored to grace and was able to continue administering the sacraments validly. The Donatists believed that the entire sacramental system of the Catholic Church had become corrupted. The *traditores* therefore needed to be replaced with people who had remained firm in their faith under persecution. Donatists also demanded the rebaptism and reordination of all those who had been baptized and ordained by *traditores*. Augustine, however, intervened, emphasizing the sinfulness of Christians. He argued that the church is not a society of saints but a mixed body of saints and sinners. Augustine refused to weed out those who had lapsed under persecution or for other reasons. The validity of the church's ministry and preaching did not depend upon the holiness of its ministers, but upon the person of Jesus Christ. The personal unworthiness of a minister did not compromise the validity of the sacraments. This view, which rapidly became normative within the church, has had a deep impact upon Christian thinking about the nature of the church and its ministers.[54]

Augustine argued against the Donatists' demand for holy ministers, as the ministers were no more holy or morally pure than anyone else, and if the power of the sacraments depended on their virtue, then no one could be certain of God's saving grace. The sacraments are worldly signs of God's efficacious grace, whether or not the minister is worthy.[55] The

---

53. Alister E. McGrath, *Historical Theology: An Introduction to the History of Christian Thought* (Malden, MA: Blackwell, 1998), 34.

54. McGrath, *Historical Theology*, 34.

55. Serene Jones and Paul Lakeland, eds., *Constructive Theology: A Contemporary Approach to Classical Themes* (Minneapolis: Fortress Press, 2005), 212.

Donatist debate brought to the forefront the questions of sacraments and ordination, which continued to be raised throughout church history.

Baptism, too, has been a contentious issue in church history. Who can be baptized and the mode of baptism were central issues, for example, in the founding of Baptists, who contended baptism was properly conducted by immersion and only for believers—those who had knowingly themselves professed Jesus as Lord. In Acts, when Paul and Silas are freed from prison, the jailer asks them, "Sirs, what must I do to be saved?" (Acts 16:30). They reply, "Believe in the Lord Jesus, and you will be saved, you and your household" (Acts 16:31). The passage ends, "then he and his entire family were baptized without delay" (Acts 16:33). This biblical reference to the "household" called for inclusion of children and infants. The entire household during the early church period included infants, children, servants, and slaves. It included everyone in the house. This led to the practice of infant baptism in most denominations. Today we must also ask whom the church includes and whom it excludes from baptism. And we must ask what baptism means in light of intersectionality's aims of justice and inclusion. In many ways, the both/and and inclusive thinking of intersectionality call the church to reimagine what baptism means in light of social differences and other faiths. Is a practice of baptism possible that invites believers into community without serving as a boundary against people of other faith? Can baptism serve as a mechanism to welcome people into a community that is unbounded? Certainly intersectionality demands that the church be reflective as it practices baptism so that baptism is not a ritual that reinforces hierarchies and structures of power but is rather a welcome and a challenge to join an inclusive community of justice and love.

Similarly, the church can use communion to mark clear boundaries around who is inside and outside the community. Many churches practice a form of closed communion, from demanding participants be baptized Christians to requiring them to be members of the local church where they take communion. Intersectional theology asks us to interrogate the practice of communion and question the meanings of the boundaries it may create. As with the practice of baptism, intersectional theology challenges us to reimagine communion as an inclusive practice that both affirms the community of believers and affirms our welcome of others. It also asks us to examine the impact of the siloing of the church. What does it mean when communion is practiced as a gathering of people who are mostly of the same race, the same social class, the same sexual identities, the same nation of origin, the same first language? When people with disabilities or older people are invisible? When women and

LGBTQ people are excluded from leadership? When children are not present? Again, Natalie K. Watson notes that the church's sacraments are uniquely embodied practices of faith.[56] Intersectional theology urges us to ask what it means, then, when so many actual human bodies are excluded or marginalized in the practice of the sacraments.

ORDINATION

Ordination has certainly been a contentious practice. The exclusion of women and LGBTQ people from ordination in most churches has been the most blatant example of the church's ongoing oppressive practice in identifying and consecrating leaders. Other forms of exclusion, however, have been subtler but just as oppressive. Churches that ordain women seldom call them as senior pastors. Even fewer churches call LGBTQ pastors. The theological understanding of ordination in many traditions sets ministers apart from laypeople in hierarchical relationships that privilege the ordained. Because churches tend to be ethnic silos, churches also tend to have pastors that are part of the dominant ethnic group.

Kwok Pui-lan notes that Asian churches have also perpetuated male dominance in their exclusion of women from ordination. She points out that those women who are ordained do not receive the same recognition or compensation as their male peers, and often, because churches do not call them, they simply have to start their own churches.[57] Lily Kuo Wang draws on the Reformed tradition of the priesthood of believers to assert that ordained ministry must be open to all.[58] Kwok emphasizes that Asian women do not seek ordination to obtain admission into the old boys' club. Rather, they seek "to enlarge the church's vision of ministry, to experiment with new models of leadership and to subvert the patriarchal church."[59]

As early as the late 1960s, Elisabeth Schüssler Fiorenza argued that simply including women among the ordained would not necessarily challenge the inherently hierarchical and patriarchal structures of the Catholic Church. She contended that only a transformation of the church itself could bring about women's equality in the church.[60]

56. Watson, *Introducing Feminist Ecclesiologies*, 80.
57. Kwok Pui-lan, *Introducing Asian Feminist Theology* (Cleveland: Pilgrim, 2000), 100.
58. Lily Kuo Wang, "Ecclesiology and Women: A View from Taiwan," in *We Dare to Dream: Doing Theology as Asian Women*, ed. Virginia Fabella and Sun Ai Lee Park (Maryknoll, NY: Orbis, 1989), 24–32.
59. Kwok, *Introducing Asian Feminist Theology*, 108.
60. Elisabeth Schüssler Fiorenza, *Discipleship of Equals: A Critical Feminist Ekklesia-ology of Liberation* (New York: Herder & Herder, 1993), 31.

Similarly, Marcella Althaus-Reid claims that "the symbolic patriarchal theological text always precedes [women]," making the enterprise of simple inclusion or "sameness equality" fruitless in the pursuit of ordination in the untransformed church.[61]

An intersectional theology of ordination challenges our notions of the meanings of ordination, as well as the practices of inclusion and exclusion of various people from ordination. In intersectional theology, ordination must be a practice of justice, directed at social transformation toward justice. Ordination reflects and reinforces the power structures of the church and, as such, has contributed to the maintenance of the dominance of white heterosexual men in the church and the continuance of white supremacist heteropatriarchy in society. Intersectional theology challenges the practice of ordination as a process that reinforces hierarchy and exclusion and calls for ordination to transform the church and the people who serve it and the world.

WORSHIP

On the one hand, worship should be a gathering of community in the presence of God and one another to share in prayer, proclamation, support, and the rituals of the church. On the other hand, worship may be the time when alienation and otherness can be most acutely felt by those outside the dominant norms of whiteness, maleness, and heterosexuality. Intersectional thinking calls the church to examine its practices of worship to root out those places that mark difference for exclusion. For example, the language of the church in the US largely reflects white heteropatriarchal norms. God is Father, Lord, Master. Jesus is the bridegroom, the church the bride. Our souls are black with sin but can be washed white as snow. In most churches, the leadership that congregants see is male, gender-conforming, heterosexual, and able-bodied. The messages of normativity are clear. Intersectional thinking asks the church to imagine new language and new leadership that reflects the aspirations of an intersectional church.

Furthermore, intersectional thinking challenges the church's emphasis on the internal and individual. A great deal of worship focuses on individuals' relationships with God and the personal tasks of living a godly life. Intersectional theology insists the church go farther to recognize the impact of structures of power on individuals and to call individuals to work in faith and in coalition toward justice as an act of authentic wor-

---

61. Marcella Althaus-Reid, *Indecent Theology: Theological Perversions in Sex, Gender and Politics* (New York: Routledge, 2000), 101–2.

ship. In intersectional theology, the worship of the church cannot be divorced from the work of the church toward social transformation in the world.

CONCLUSION

What might a radically transformed intersectional church look like? We can make some initial, general suggestions—it would reflect gender, racial, sexual, economic, ability, age, and national diversity in the congregation and in leadership. Its practices, from baptism to ministry, would be inclusive, open, both/and, multiple in their orientation to others within and without the church. Its mission would be directed toward justice through supporting the development of individual Christians in community and toward the broader world of which we all are a part. The details of an intersectional church will have to be worked out at the local church level with attention to the church's own history and theology, the local community in which the church ministers, and the broader social and political situations within which the church carries out its mission and ministry.

Intersectionality as a lens for ecclesiology can help the church address contemporary needs by centering awareness of intersecting individual identities within matrices of social, political, economic, and religious power. Intersectionality can also help us raise questions to challenge the church to transform itself. What might a radically reformed intersectional worship look like? Perhaps it's not Sunday morning in the pews following the liturgy. How might the church change if it centered its understanding of intersectional identities and institutional and structural power? What might the church become if we started from the ground up, with questions of difference, justice, equity, inclusion, and intersectionality at the center? What would that church look like? What might that church become in the struggle to fulfill God's kin-dom? What role could that church play in God's in-breaking community of love, peace, and justice?

QUESTIONS

1. As we reflect on our intersectional identities, how does this provide opportunities for coalitions?

2. Individualism versus community has been a source of contention for immigrants who come from non-Western countries. What can we learn from how they emphasize community over the individual?

3. What would it mean for you to center intersectionality in your faith practices? What is intersectional spirituality?

4. What steps do you need to take to learn more about people, cultures, and faiths different from your own? How might this contribute to the development of your theology?

5. What is the church for you? What would it mean for your faith community to center intersectionality in its faith practices?

6. What does intersectionality mean for how you think about church membership, church leadership, baptism, communion, and engagement? How do we build intercultural communities or ministry?

7. How does intersectionality complicate our thinking about insiders/outsiders in the Christian community?

8. What does it mean for you to imagine the church as a resistant community? How do we practice intersectionality?

6.

Conclusion

Intersectional theology is rooted in our deep awareness of and attention to identities, social structures, and power. Rather than seeing theology as pursuit of a single, consistent, and unified truth, intersectional theology embraces the theological multiplicity and indeterminacy that arises from diverse identities and social locations. Central to intersectional theology is a focused and humble cognizance of how one's own social location affects how one does theology. In other words, intersectional theology begins in a recognition that all theologies are contextualized and that contextualization matters. It reminds us that we are always present in and part of the theologies we do, and it calls us to recognize both the insights and limitations our social location brings to our theologies. In no way does that recognition invalidate the value of any individual's theological ideas, but it does draw attention to the boundaries and limitations of any or all of our theologizing. It also underscores the necessity of a wide range of theologies from diverse social locations to bring other essential experiences and perspectives into the theological conversation. In particular, intersectional theology investigates the roles of structures and power in theologizing and directs theologizing toward social justice. Intersectional theology recognizes that all people exist in different relations to social, economic, political, and religious power within the matrix of domination and that theologies from these various locations will offer us new, unexpected, and necessary viewpoints to move us toward a greater collective knowledge of God and work toward justice. By centering intersectional thinking in our theologizing, we counter the hegemony of dominant theologies that proceed from unexamined and often invisible places of social and religious power and privilege, and we open ourselves to novel, exciting, challenging, and sometimes difficult perspectives that can complicate, nuance, and enliven our theologies and can encompass and reflect a greater diversity of human experience within and across differences.

Intersectional theology offers us a powerful tool to address many of the pressing issues of the twenty-first century. In recent years, we've seen increasing divisiveness across lines of race, gender, social class, immigration status, sexuality, politics, and religion. Many of the problems giving rise to contemporary tendencies to retreat into one's own affinity groups are closely related to our propensity for single-axis thinking. We seem inclined to clasp onto our own target identities without recognizing our intersecting dominant identities and our social location in relation to power within social institutions. In fact, we even see people within dominant groups co-opting the language of oppression to deny their power and privilege and claim target status. For example, some conservative Christian businesspeople are claiming that their religious rights are being violated when the government demands they not discriminate against LGBTQ people. White Nationalists allege that white people are under threat by the advancement of people of color. Men's rights groups argue that because of the progress of women's rights men are now an oppressed group in the United States. People on the Left are not immune from this tendency either. Gay men can be misogynist. Lesbians can be transphobic. Progressive men can engage in sexual harassment. White feminists can act in racist ways. When we participate in single-axis thinking, we often perpetuate individual acts of bigotry and reinforce discriminatory systems and institutions. Intersectional thinking demands we keep in mind the multiple and intersectional axes of identity within structures of power as we consider contemporary issues such as marriage equality, reproductive justice, wealth inequality, addiction, and violence.

In the church, intersectional thinking can help us address pressing social problems with significantly deeper and more nuanced analysis and practice our faith through underpinning theologies that inspire and facilitate just action in the church and in the world. Intersectional theology calls us to start this work in our own houses, to address single-axis thinking and the perpetuation of systems of domination in the church itself. Intersectional theology helps us understand and build the church as a community of diverse people with diverse experiences, perspectives, and beliefs, committed together to work toward God's community of love, peace, and justice. Intersectional thinking helps us understand why Sunday morning at eleven is the most segregated hour in the country, why church membership is declining, why the church seems irrelevant, how the church has harmed people through beliefs and practices that do not embody the love of God toward all, why we can't seem to talk across our differences, why some Christians have abandoned their own moral convictions to support a political administration that contradicts basic Christian beliefs in honesty, compassion, and fairness. Intersectional theology also offers us a way forward, a blueprint for a different kind of theology and a different kind of church that reflects the diverse and multiple people of God in all their difference. It also gives us a goal and a method—justice. Across our differences, embracing our differences, joining together, we can be just in our means and have justice as our end. Intersectional theology reminds us of the gospel's message of liberation, inclusion, welcoming, equality, and love and demands in our theologizing and in our practice of church that we always work in that direction.

Other theologies of liberation have worked toward achieving a similar goal. Often, however, these theologies of liberation have failed to offer intersectional analysis that sees the liberation of men of color tied to the liberation of women or the liberation of women tied to the liberation of the poor, or the liberation of women of color tied to the liberation of LGBTQ people and people with disabilities. These other theologies failed to connect the multiple forms of oppressions that people experience due to their simultaneous experience of gender, ethnicity, religion, socioeconomic status, sexuality, nationality, age, and ability within systems of white, colonialist, capitalist, heteropatriarchal power. What the various forms of theology failed to recognize and address, intersectional theology tries to engage through its intentional and focused attention to intersecting identities and interlocking systems of oppression. It moves toward an intercultural church and intersectional ecclesiology that fully embraces all people and works toward justice within and across all groups of people. It moves us toward a resistant church that goes against dominating powers that continue to marginalize, subjugate, and subordinate people based on their social location within the matrix of power and privilege.

Intersectional theology is complicated. It's difficult because it calls us to be aware of our intersecting dominant and subordinate identities within structures of power. It demands that we not approach theology through a single axis. It convicts us of our own personal participation in social injustices as we fail to recognize that categories intersect and overlap each other. It reminds us that no one of us is the arbiter of truth or faith. Yet intersectional theology moves us toward a more inclusive and accurate understanding of the full human experience, especially as it embraces and highlights the "least of these," those whom theology often ignores or marginalizes—the poor, people of color, women, people from the Two-Thirds World, immigrants, LGBTQ people, people with disabilities, older people, people of different faiths or no faith—all of these, across all of their differences—become central in intersectional theology. No one is left out or left behind in our theologizing. And our theologizing becomes a vehicle for social, political, economic, and religious transformation in the world. Intersectional theology is not simply another theological method, a side note to traditional theology. It is a necessity for all who do theology if we are to ensure our theologies are inclusive, just, and relevant to the in-breaking kin-dom of God.

We envision a world where all are accepted in our homes, our churches, and our societies. We envision a church characterized by full inclusion, a church in which people are not discriminated against or excluded because of their sexuality, gender, race, ethnicity, class, ability, national origin, immigration status, or first language. Our hope for the world is that we are all welcomed into the kin-dom of God and we can live in peace with each other. Our hope for crafting an intersectional theology is that churches and faith communities can embrace it as a way to live out the reign of God on earth. In other words, intersectional theology is not a theoretical and philosophical concept or set of ideas but a lived theology and an embodied reality.

Finally, intersectional theology is a theology of hope. It encourages us to see the world through a different lens and pushes us out of our comfort zones. It is a theology for the present and the future. As we recognize our lives intersecting and intertwining, intersectional theology challenges us to move toward embrace rather than suspicion of one another. It pushes us to build a movement toward love, hope, and peace rather than hurt, division, separation, and pain. It calls us to transform structures of power and create an equitable and just world that reflects the inclusive faith and love of Jesus. We believe such a world is possible and we can participate in creating that world. If each of us takes part in the intersectional enterprise, recognizes that our lives are intersecting possibilities of hope and love, and commits to a vision of radical love and justice that transforms church and society, then we can all work together toward building such a future.

QUESTIONS

1. How can intersectional theology help you address pressing faith, community, and global issues?
2. Intersectional theology is complicated and messy. Are you ready to apply it to your theological reflection and discourse? Does it provide hope for you in a broken world?
3. What is your vision for a just world?
4. How can intersectional theology help us maintain hope in the face of injustice and oppression?

Glossary

Both/And: Rather than an either/or approach to theology, a both/and approach, described by Vivian May, encourages an embrace of nuance, interconnections, complicated relationships, fluidity, and even contradiction.

Bracket: To set aside one's own beliefs and assumptions in order to enter into the logics of other claims.

Colonialism: When a group or nation seeks control of another people or nation. In most cases to exploit the land, resources, people, and heritage.

Difference: Socially constructed binaries that confer dominance or subordination on group members (gender, race, social class, ability, sexual identity, age, religion, country of origin). In other words, difference is those identities that get assigned to us in such a way that they affect how others interact with us and how we interact with the world. Based on which identity is assigned to us, we are put in a place in the social hierarchy. That place is complicated by the way differences intersect.

Feminism: bell hooks defines feminism as a movement to end sexist oppression.[1]

Gender: The ways people perform socially constructed masculine or feminine behaviors/identities.

---

1. bell hooks, *Feminism Is for Everybody: Passionate Politics* (Cambridge, MA: South End Press, 2000).

Gender-First: An analytical approach that gives priority to gender over other intersecting facets of identity, such as race or sexuality.

Gender Identity: An individual's own sense of gender, which may or may not match the gender assigned at birth.

Han: A Korean term that is often translated as "unjust suffering." Everyone suffers, but oppressive systems such as sexism and racism create "unjust suffering." The pain experienced in *han* is often described as "piercing of the heart" and "deep woundedness in the heart." Korean American theologians use the term "*han*" to describe the Asian American experience of racism, oppression, and marginalization.

Hermeneutics of Indeterminacy: An interpretive approach that fosters multiple and sometimes conflicting readings of a text.

Hybridity: Hybridity is about mixture, and, according to Robert Young, hybridity brings together and fuses but also maintains separation. Hybridity tries to create new spaces and places of discourse. Hybridity makes difference into sameness and sameness into difference, but in a way that makes the same no longer the same, the different no longer simply different.[2]

Imperialism: The political and economic dominance of one nation over another. Imperialism tries to create an empire by conquering another's land and state. There is some similarity between imperialism and colonialism. Imperialism involves the practice of one dominating group over a distant land while colonialism is about establishing settlements on a distant land. Imperialism includes colonialism, but colonialism does not always include imperialism.

Indecent Theology: A form of liberation theology that includes the critical approaches of gender, queer, and postcolonial theories. It seeks to work toward liberating sexuality from heterosexual norms.

Intercultural Theology: A theology that pays attention to the identity of non-European Christianity in dialogue with Western forms. It uses insights from sociocultural, interfaith dialogue, and history to understand the interaction of people across ethnicities and nationalities and God's presence in their lives.

---

2. Robert J. C. Young, *Colonial Desire: Hybridity in Theory, Culture and Race* (London: Routledge, 1995), 22, 26.

Intersectionality: Coined by Kimberlé Crenshaw, a tool for analysis and a problem-solving approach, biased toward justice, that holds multifaceted identities and systems of oppression in mind as simultaneous and mutually shaping forces that situate people differently within the matrix of domination.

Liberation Theology: Liberation theology arose in the 1960s with a focus on the poor and the political liberation of oppressed people. The father of liberation theology is usually understood as Gustavo Gutiérrez of Peru, who understands poverty as a condition and emphasizes a "preferential option for the poor."

Matrix of Domination: Coined by Patricia Hill Collins, the organization of power, the means by which intersecting oppressions are regulated through social institutions such as the family, government, education, and religion.

***Minjung* Theology**: A theology that emerged in the 1970s in Korea due to the oppressed experiences of South Korean Christians. The word *minjung* means "people," and *minjung* theology is a theology that seeks to liberate. Most recently, *minjung* theology focuses on the reunification of North and South Korea.

Mujerista Theology: A US Latina theology that focuses on liberating Latina women from sexism, racism, and economic oppression. It is a theology that describes Latinas' role in their struggle for liberation and freedom and works to enable Latinas to gain economic, social, and political freedom.

Mythical Norm: The accumulation of dominant identities to which accrues social, political, and economic power. Audre Lorde identifies this norm in US culture as "white, thin, male, young, heterosexual, Christian, and financially secure."[3]

Oppression: Marilyn Frye traces the meaning of oppression to its root word, *to press*, to be caught between systematically related and interlocking barriers that constrain or prevent mobility.[4] Suzanne Pharr explains that oppressions (sexism, racism, heterosexism, etc.) share a number

---

3. Audre Lorde, "Age, Race, Class, and Sex: Women Redefining Difference," in *Sister Outsider: Essays & Speeches by Audre Lorde*, 2nd ed. (New York: Crossing Press, 2007), 116.
4. Marilyn Frye, *The Politics of Reality: Essays in Feminist Theory* (New York: Crossing Press, 1983).

of common elements: defined norms, institutional power, economic power, threats of violence, lack of prior claim, othering, invisibility, stereotyping, victim-blaming, horizontal hostility, isolation, assimilation, tokenism, and individual solutions.[5]

Postcolonial Feminism: Postcolonial feminism emerged in the 1980s as a critique of the universalization of Western feminism and the misrepresentation of women in non-Western countries. Postcolonial feminism understands that racism, politics, socioeconomic context, and culture all have an effect on nonwhite women in the postcolonial world.

Power: Typically defined as "power-over," the ability to coerce another's behavior. Power also includes access to social, political, and economic resources. In systems of oppression, power accrues to those who most closely approximate the mythical norm—(in the United States) male, white, heterosexual, financially stable, young-middle adult, able-bodied, Christian. Social institutions (family, education, religion, media, government) reproduce hierarchy and ensure the maintenance of power in the hands of members of the dominant culture by normalizing the dominant culture so that hierarchical orderings based on gender, race, social class, and so forth appear natural and inevitable.

Praxis: An action-reflection model that engages participants in an ongoing loop of active participation in making social change and reflection/theorizing based on that experience that leads to more effective action.

Privilege: Peggy McIntosh defines privilege as "an invisible package of unearned assets." Privilege is those social goods we receive, not through work or merit, but through our membership in dominant groups. For example, white privilege means white people can go shopping alone and move about the store fairly well assured that they will not be followed by store detectives because of their race.

Process Theology: Process theology arose from process philosophy, which was developed by Alfred North Whitehead (1861–1947). John Cobb, a noted process theologian, states that "process theology may refer to all forms of theology that emphasize event, occurrence, or becoming over against substance."[6]

---

5. Suzanne Pharr, *Homophobia: A Weapon of Sexism* (Little Rock, AR: Women's Project, 1988).

6. John B. Cobb Jr., *Process Theology as Political Theology* (Manchester, UK: Manchester University Press, 1982), 19.

Queer Theology: Queer theology tries to erase and deconstruct boundaries on sexual and gender identity by reclaiming gender nonconformity and lesbian, gay, bisexual, and queer sexuality as part of human history. Queer theology questions social and cultural norms regarding gender and sexuality, especially as they are assumed and applied within theology.

Race: A socially constructed category by which people perceive themselves and are perceived by others as sharing distinctive biological and hereditary traits.

Racism: A system of oppression (as opposed to an individual attitude of bigotry) that confers differential social, economic, and political advantage based on perceptions of biological differences among so-called racial groups.

Resistance: The refusal to be complicit with oppression. People resist through consciousness-raising, nonviolent protest, noncooperation, interrupting oppressive behavior, activism, art, humor, music, survival, and other modes of challenge to dominant systems.

Sexism: The system of oppression (as opposed to individual attitudes of bigotry) that assigns people to one of two gender categories, ranks men/maleness/masculinity over women/femaleness/femininity, and then confers social, political, and economic advantage on men.

Single-Axis Thinking: Using only one axis of identity (gender or race or class) for analysis.

Slippages: Movements from intersectional thinking back to single-axis thinking.

Social Justice: A structuring of institutions and relationships so that people's basic needs are met, people are treated with equity and fairness, differences are welcomed and valued, and economic, social, political, and religious equality is achieved.

Social Location: An individual's place in relation to social, political, and economic power based on interlocking categories of identity such as gender, race, class, sexual identity, religion, nation of origin, age, and ability.

Systems of Oppression: Mutually constitutive and interlocking arrangements of social, economic, and political power rooted in gender, race, social class, ability, age, nation of origin, sexual identity, and religion.

Transgender: Gender identity/expression that crosses traditional expectations of the gender assigned at birth.

Transnational Feminism: Feminist theory and practice that recognizes the interconnecting impacts of colonialism, globalism, and capitalism on the lives of women, particularly women of color and other marginalized people around the world.

Two-Thirds World: In contrast to the First World, or developed world, Two-Thirds World recognizes that the majority of the world's people still live in conditions of poverty, conflict, and colonial legacy.

Womanism: Coined by Alice Walker, theories and practices of liberation informed by black women's experiences and thought.

Xenophobia: Fear of the stranger or an attitude of hostility toward people who are not natives in a particular situation, usually foreigners.

Bibliography

Althaus-Reid, Marcella. *Indecent Theology: Theological Perversions in Sex, Gender and Politics.* New York: Routledge, 2000.
Aquino, Maria Pilar. *Feminist Intercultural Theology: Latina Explorations for a Just World.* Maryknoll, NY: Orbis, 2007.
Bhabha, Homi. *The Location of Culture.* London: Routledge, 1994.
Cheng, Patrick S. "Rethinking Sin and Grace for LGBT People Today." In *Sexuality and the Sacred: Sources for Theological Reflection*, edited by Marvin M. Ellison and Kelly Brown Douglas. 2nd ed. Louisville: Westminster John Knox, 2010.
Chung, Hyun Kyung. *Struggle to Be the Sun Again: Introducing Asian Women's Theology.* Maryknoll, NY: Orbis, 1990.
Cole, Johnetta Betsch, and Beverly Guy-Sheftall. *Gender Talk: The Struggle for Women's Equality in African American Communities.* New York: Ballantine, 2003.
Coleman, Monica. *Making a Way out of No Way: A Womanist Theology.* Minneapolis: Fortress Press, 2008.
Collins, Patricia Hill, and Sirma Bilge. *Intersectionality.* Cambridge, UK: Polity, 2016.
Combahee River Collective. "A Black Feminist Statement." In *Words of Fire: An Anthology of African-American Feminist Thought.* Edited by Beverly Guy-Sheftall. New York: New Press, 1995.
Cornwall, Susannah. "Apophasis and Ambiguity: The 'Unknowingness' of Transgender." In *Trans/Formations*, edited by Marcella Althaus-Reid and Lisa Isherwood. London: SCM, 2009.
Cox, Harvey. *On Not Leaving It to the Snake.* New York: Macmillan, 1967.
Daggers, Jenny, and Grace Ji-Sun Kim, eds. *Christian Doctrines for Global Gender Justice.* New York: Palgrave Macmillan, 2015.
Davis, Angela. *Women, Culture, Politics.* New York: Vintage, 1989.

Douglas, Kelly Brown. *The Black Christ.* Maryknoll, NY: Orbis, 1994.
———. *Sexuality and the Black Church.* New York: Orbis, 1999.
———. *Stand Your Ground: Black Bodies and the Justice of God.* Maryknoll, NY: Orbis, 2016.
Dube, Musa, ed. *Other Ways of Reading: African Women and the Bible.* Atlanta: Society of Biblical Literature, 2001.
Duncan, Celena. "The Book of Ruth: On Boundaries, Love, and Truth." In *Take Back the Word*, edited by Robert Goss and Mona West. Cleveland: Pilgrim, 2000.
Fabella, Virginia, and Sun Ai Lee Park, eds. *We Dare to Dream: Doing Theology as Asian Women.* Maryknoll, NY: Orbis, 1989.
Fulkerson, Mary McClintock. *Changing the Subject: Women's Discourses and Feminist Theology.* Minneapolis: Fortress, 1994.
Goss, Robert, and Mona West. Introduction to *Take Back the Word*. Cleveland: Pilgrim, 2000.
Gutiérrez, Gustavo. *A Theology of Liberation.* Maryknoll, NY: Orbis 1990.
Hancock, Ange-Marie. *Intersectionality: An Intellectual History.* New York: Oxford University Press, 2016.
Hinson-Hasty, Elizabeth. *The Problem of Wealth: A Christian Response to a Culture of Affluence.* Maryknoll, NY: Orbis, 2017.
hooks, bell. *Feminist Theory: From Margin to Center.* 2nd ed. Cambridge, MA: South End Press, 2000.
Isherwood, Lisa. *Introducing Feminist Christologies.* Cleveland: Pilgrim, 2002.
———. *Liberating Christ.* Cleveland: Pilgrim, 1999.
Johnson, Elizabeth A. *Quest for the Living God: Mapping Frontiers in the Theology of God.* New York: Continuum, 2007.
Jones, Serene, and Paul Lakeland, eds. *Constructive Theology: A Contemporary Approach to Classical Themes.* Minneapolis: Fortress Press, 2005.
Kim, Grace Ji-Sun. *Embracing the Other: The Transformative Spirit of Love.* Grand Rapids: Eerdmans, 2015.
———. *The Grace of Sophia: A Korean North American Women's Christology.* Cleveland: Pilgrim, 2002.
———. *Holy Spirit, Chi and the Other.* New York: Palgrave Macmillan, 2011.
Kim, Grace Ji-Sun, and Jann Aldredge-Clanton. *Intercultural Ministry: Hope for a Changing World.* Valley Forge: Judson Press, 2017.
Kim, Grace Ji-Sun, and Jenny Daggers, eds. *Reimagining with Christian Doctrines.* New York: Palgrave Macmillan, 2014.
Kim, Kirsteen. *The Holy Spirit in the World: A Global Conversation.* Maryknoll, NY: Orbis, 2007.

King, Martin Luther, Jr. *Stride toward Freedom: The Montgomery Story*. Manhattan: Harper & Brothers, 1958.
King, Ursula, ed. *Feminist Theology from the Third World: A Reader*. Eugene, OR: Wipf & Stock, 1994.
Kwok, Pui-lan. *Hope Abundant: Third World and Indigenous Women's Theology*. Maryknoll, NY: Orbis, 2010.
———. *Introducing Asian Feminist Theology*. Cleveland: Pilgrim, 2000.
———. *Postcolonial Imagination and Feminist Theology*. Louisville: Westminster John Knox, 2005.
Lee, Hyo-Dong. *Spirit, Qi, and the Multitude: A Comparative Theology for the Democracy of Creation*. New York: Fordham University Press, 2014.
Lee, Jung Young. *God Suffers for Us: A Systematic Inquiry into a Concept of Divine Passibility*. Netherlands: Martinus Nyhoff, 1974.
Lightsey, Pamela R. *Our Lives Matter: A Womanist Queer Theology*. Eugene, OR: Pickwick, 2015.
Lorde, Audre. "Age, Race, Class, and Sex: Women Redefining Difference." In *Sister Outsider: Essays & Speeches*. 2nd ed. New York: Crossing Press, 2007.
———, eds. "There Is No Hierarchy of Oppressions." In *I Am Your Sister: Collected and Unpublished Writings of Audre Lorde*. Edited by Johnetta Betsch and Beverly Guy-Sheftall. New York: Oxford University Press, 2009.
May, Vivian M. *Pursuing Intersectionality: Unsettling Dominant Imaginaries*. New York: Routledge, 2015.
McGrath, Alister. *Christian Theology: An Introduction*. Oxford: Blackwell, 1994.
McKnight, Edgar V. *Jesus Christ in History and Scripture: A Poetic and Sectarian Perspective*. Macon, GA: Mercer University Press, 1999.
Mitchem, Stephanie. *Introducing Womanist Theology*. Maryknoll: Orbis, 2002.
Oduyoye, Mercy Amba. *African Women's Theology*. Cleveland: Pilgrim, 2001.
Pungar, Joseph. *Theology Interpreted*. Lanham, MD: University Press of America, 1993.
Schüssler Fiorenza, Elisabeth. *Discipleship of Equals: A Critical Feminist Ekklesiaology of Liberation*. New York: Herder & Herder, 1993.
———. *The Power of the Word: Scripture and the Rhetoric of Empire*. Minneapolis: Fortress Press, 2007.
———. *Sharing Her Word: Feminist Biblical Interpretation in Context*. Boston: Beacon, 1998.
Smith, Barbara. "Homophobia: Why Bring It Up?" In *The Truth That Never Hurts: Writings on Race, Gender, and Freedom*. New Brunswick, NJ: Rutgers University Press, 1998.
Trible, Phyllis. *Texts of Terror: Literary-Feminist Readings of Biblical Narratives*. Minneapolis: Fortress Press, 1984.

Watson, Natalie K. *Introducing Feminist Ecclesiology*. Eugene, OR: Wipf & Stock, 1996.

Williams, Delores S. *Sisters in the Wilderness: The Challenge of Womanist God-Talk*. Maryknoll, NY: Orbis, 2013.

Wilson, Nancy. *Our Tribe: Queer Folks, God, Jesus, and the Bible*. San Francisco: HarperCollins, 1995.

Woodley, Randy S. *Shalom and the Community of Creation: An Indigenous Vision*. Grand Rapids: Eerdmans, 2012.

Young, Robert. *Colonial Desire: Hybridity in Theory, Culture and Race*. London: Routledge, 1995.

Index

ableism/ability, xi, xiv, xv, xvii, xix, 2, 18, 19, 38, 41, 45, 68, 76, 79–81, 87, 95, 98, 105, 109, 110, 113, 117, 118
abortion, 58, 86
Africa, 27, 54, 72, 83, 101
African, 42, 51, 54, 61, 70, 72, 91, 101, 120, 121
African-American, 30, 71, 87–88, 90, 97, 120
against the grain, 12, 14, 59–60
Ainsworth United Church of Christ, 96–97
Aldredge-Clanton, Jann, 88, 120
Althaus-Reid, Marcella, 46, 60, 87, 104, 119
Anselm, 60, 66
Anzaldúa, Gloria, 6
Aquino, Maria Pilar, 87, 119
Asia, 27, 47, 83, 89
Asian, xi, 23, 24, 31, 32, 42, 48, 54, 57, 61, 70, 77, 82, 89, 103, 120, 121
Asian American, xvii, 6, 31, 38, 46, 48, 54, 80, 114
Augustine, 38, 50, 60, 101

Baptism, xii, xix, 79, 100–102, 105–6

Baptist, xvii, 26–29, 37, 49, 102
Barth, Karl, 14
Beal, Francis, 4
Bell, Lynn, 93–94
Bhabha, Homi, 88, 119
bias toward justice, 10, 20, 39, 44–45, 64, 68, 75, 86
Bible, 14, 25, 47, 54, 65, 70–77, 82, 120, 122
Bilge, Sirma, 3, 7–10, 79–80, 119
Biography, xvii, 19
Black, 4, 5, 26, 92, 96–97, 104
Blacks, 99
Black bodies, 56, 59, 120
Black Christ, 45, 120
black church, 6, 81, 90–91, 96, 120
black community, 81
black lesbians, 73
black liberation, xvi
black theology, 38, 45, 72
black women, xii, xvii, 1–5, 16, 48, 61, 91, 96, 118
body/bodies, 56–57, 59, 91, 103, 120
Bong, Sharon A., 57
both/and, xii, 7, 9, 11, 18–19, 38, 40, 53–54, 58, 64, 67–68, 82, 84, 92, 95, 98, 102, 105, 113
bracket, 43, 83, 93, 95, 113

Canaanite woman, xv, xviii
Capitalism, xiv, 47–48, 50, 95, 98, 118
Catholic, 85, 101, 103
Cheng, Patrick, xviii, 48, 119
Chi, 69–70, 77, 120
Class, xi, xiii, xv, xvii, xviii, 2, 4–7, 9–10, 13, 16, 18–20, 22, 24, 26, 34–35, 38, 41–42, 44–46, 58–60, 63, 68, 71–76, 80–82, 86–87, 91, 98, 102, 108, 110, 113, 115–18, 121
Classism, xvii, xix, 38, 72, 79, 80, 82, 95
Christology, 51, 54, 67, 77, 91, 120
Chung Hyun Kyung, xviii, 47–48, 119
Church, xii, xiii, xv, xvi, xvii, xviii, xix, 6, 16, 18, 23–32, 37, 42, 49–52, 54, 56–57, 59–61, 63, 67–70, 76, 79, 81–82, 84–106, 108–110
Clarke, Cheryl, 6
Coalition, xiv, 7, 10, 12, 79, 80–81, 104, 106
Coleman, Monica, 45, 119
Collins, Patricia Hill, xiii, xiv, xvi, 3, 5–10, 73, 79–80, 115, 119
Collusion, 28, 62–63, 93, 95
Colonial/colonialism, xv, 7, 14, 36, 38, 42, 46–47, 51, 53, 62, 64, 70, 72, 76, 86, 87, 95, 109, 113, 114, 118, 122
Combahee River Collective, xiii, 4, 12
Communion, xix, 79, 87, 100, 102–3
Community, xii, xiii, xviii, xix, 2, 5, 6, 13, 18, 23, 51–53, 58, 73, 79, 80, 83–84, 87–92, 94, 97–100, 102, 104–6, 108, 111, 122
Complexity, xvi, 10, 16, 53, 67, 73, 76
Context/contextual, xii, xiii, xvii, xviii, 6, 10, 13–17, 21, 29, 36, 38–39, 41–42, 44, 46, 48, 50–52, 58, 60, 68, 70–72, 75, 80, 89, 91–92, 94, 107, 116, 121
Contraception, 58, 86
Cooper, Anna Julia, xiii, 1, 4
countermemory, 12
Cornwall, Susannah, 59–60, 119
Cox, Harvey, 94, 119
Crenshaw, Kimberle, xvi, 1, 2, 80–81, 115

Davis, Angela, 6, 10, 119
decolonize, 47, 62, 70
DeGraffenried v General Motors, 1
Descartes, 66
desegregated, 25
diakonia, 97–98
discrimination, xiv, 1, 2, 5, 34, 37, 63, 81, 83, 94
discourse, 11–12
diverse/diversity, xi, xiii, xv–xviii, 3–4, 6–7, 16, 33–34, 38, 41–44, 53, 60–62, 64, 67–68, 76, 80, 84, 86–89, 97, 105, 107–9
dominance, xiii–xiv, xviii, 4, 7, 19, 44, 46, 55, 76, 81, 86, 95, 103–4, 113, 115
domination, xi, xii, xiii, xiv, xviii, 5–7, 11, 18, 34, 51–52, 70–71, 80, 82, 84, 92–93, 107–8, 115
Donatist, 100–102
Douglas, Kelly Brown, 45, 48, 59, 81, 119, 120
Dube, Musa, 7, 70, 72, 74, 120
Duncan, Celena, 74, 120

ecclesiology, xii, 89–92, 95, 100, 103, 105, 109, 122
either/or, 7, 9, 11, 18, 58, 67, 82, 113
Ekejuiba, Felicia I., 91
empire, 47, 61, 71, 114, 121
epistemological/epistemology, 8, 10–11, 44, 47
eschatology, 56, 58
ethics/ethical, 45, 63
Ethiopian eunuch, xv, xviii
Ethnicity, xviii, 2, 18, 23, 46, 48, 63, 68, 74–76, 80, 87–88, 109–10
equity, xix, 2, 15, 34, 58, 81, 105, 117, 124
evangelical, 28, 62, 85
experience, ix, xi–xiii, xv–xviii, 1–4, 6, 8, 11–13, 18–23, 25, 27–28, 30, 38–45, 47–49, 51–53, 57, 59–60, 63–64, 67–68, 72–74, 80–82, 90–92, 94, 96, 99, 100, 107, 109, 114–16, 118

faith, xii–xiii, xvi, xix, 21, 31, 34, 36, 38, 43, 49, 53, 55, 65, 68, 72, 79, 81, 83–85, 88, 90, 94, 97, 98, 101–4, 106, 108–11, 114
feminist/feminism, ix, xi–xvii, 1–2, 4–6, 8, 10, 13, 18, 28, 32, 38, 41, 42, 44–56, 62, 64, 68, 70–74, 87, 89–91, 100, 103, 108, 113, 115, 116, 118–22; black, xii
feminist theology, 32, 44–48, 50, 52, 54, 62, 68, 89–91, 103, 120
feminization of poverty, 99
Fiorenza, Elisabeth Schüssler, xviii, 42, 44, 71, 103, 121
Fulkerson, Mary McClintock, 53–54, 120

Gebara, Ivone 52
Gedalof, Irene 11
gender xi, xiii, xiv–xv, xvii, 6–11, 13–16, 18, 19, 24, 28, 29, 35, 38, 41, 42, 44–46, 48, 50–54, 58, 60–64, 68, 70–76, 79–81, 86, 87, 90–99, 104–5, 108–10, 113–14, 116, 117–119, 121, 124
gender-first 114
gender identity xv, 16, 53, 81, 114, 117–18
gender justice 61–62, 119
Goss, Robert 73–74, 120
Gutierrez, Gustavo 94–95, 115, 120
Guy-Sheftall, Beverly xvii, 4–6, 119, 120

Hagar, 71
han, xii, 35–36, 38, 40, 114
Hancock, Ange-Marie, xvi, 3–4, 7–8, 14, 120
Harris, Duchess, 12
hearth-hold, 91
hemorrhaging woman, xv, xviii, 72
hermeneutics, 29, 42, 51, 114
heterosexuality, xiv, 35, 59, 104
heterosexism, xvii, xix, 4–5, 8, 45, 79, 95, 115
hierarchy/hierarchical, xix, 2, 5, 8, 11–12, 15–16, 21, 37, 41, 46, 52, 75, 85, 103–4, 113, 116, 119
historical criticism, 75
hokmah, 54, 67
Holy Spirit, 14, 61, 69–70, 98, 120
homophobia, 8, 35, 45, 75, 80–82, 86, 95, 116, 121
hope, xiii, xix, 51–52, 54, 57, 61, 88, 110–11, 120, 121
Hopkins, Dwight, 88
hooks, bell, xvii, 6, 8, 113, 120

hybridity, 69, 87–88, 90, 114, 122

identity, xi, xiii, xv, xviii, 2–5, 8, 11, 13, 16–19, 22–23, 27, 35–36, 38, 41–42, 44–45, 48–51, 53, 63, 66–68, 70, 72, 74, 76, 79–83, 85, 87, 89, 108, 113–14, 117–18
immigrant/immigration, xvii, 20–22, 24, 31, 35, 74, 86, 99, 106, 108, 110
imperialism, xiv, 38, 47, 50–51, 70, 72, 114
indecent theology, 46, 87, 104, 114, 119
individual, xiii, xviii, xix, 2, 9, 15–16, 19, 21, 27–28, 33, 35–36, 38–39, 43, 48, 50–52, 79, 84, 88, 97, 98, 104–8, 114, 116–17
inequality, xiv, 4, 6, 7, 9, 10, 55, 63, 108
intercultural, 61, 69, 77, 87–89, 106, 109, 119–20
interlocking, ix, xi, xviii, xix, 4, 9, 13, 17, 19, 41, 45, 55, 70, 79–80, 95, 109, 115, 117–18
intersectional theology, xii, xiii, xv–xix, 2–3, 9, 16–17, 19–21, 36, 38–47, 49–50, 53, 55–60, 62–64, 67–69, 76–77, 79, 88–89, 96–98, 102–5, 107–11
intersections, xii, xiv–xviii, 1, 4–13, 15, 19–21, 24, 38–39, 41, 44–46, 48–51, 53, 55, 59, 63, 68, 70, 72–75, 83–87, 90–92, 95, 98
intersectionality, ix, xi–xviii, 1–4, 6–15, 17–18, 20–21, 39–41, 43, 49, 63, 65, 67–71, 74–76, 79, 81–84, 86, 88, 92, 95–100, 102, 105–6, 115, 119–121
Isasi Dias, Ada Maria, xviii, 45
Isherwood, Lisa, 2, 51, 55–56, 58, 60, 119, 120

Jesus xiii, xv, xviii, 14, 26, 32, 42, 51, 54, 58, 66–67, 69, 73–75, 82, 88, 93–95, 98–99, 101–2, 104, 110, 121–22
Johnson, Elizabeth A. xviii, 90, 120

ki 69
Kim, Grace Ji-Sun v, 50, 54, 56, 61, 67, 69, 74, 88, 119–21
King, Martin Luther Jr. 82, 121
Kinukawa, Hisako 42
Koinonia 92, 97, 99
Kwok, Pui Lan xviii, 7, 46, 47, 51–52, 54, 57, 61–62, 74, 89–90, 103, 121

language, 23, 25, 35, 47, 55, 60, 83, 96–97, 102, 104, 108, 110
Latin American, xiii, 13, 38, 42, 46, 52
leadership, 25, 29, 31, 81, 84, 86, 96, 100, 103–6
Lee, Hyo-Dong, 61, 121
Lee, Jung Young, 66, 121
lesbian, xvii, 5, 20, 34, 48, 73, 80, 82, 91, 108, 117
LGBTQ, xiv, xvi, 3, 55, 80, 81, 85–87, 90, 93–94, 96, 97, 99, 100, 103, 108, 109–10
liberation/liberatory, ix, xii–xviii, 5, 7, 8, 13, 38, 42, 44, 46, 51–52, 55, 57–58, 64, 67–68, 70–72, 79, 82, 90, 93–95, 103, 109, 114–15, 118, 120–21

liberation theology, xii, 13, 38, 46, 94, 114–15
Lightsey, Pamela R., 16, 45, 73, 81, 121
logos, 67–68
Lorde, Audre, xiii, xvi, 4–5, 80, 115, 119, 121
Luther, Martin, 38, 60, 82, 121, 125

maleness, xiv, 14, 49, 59, 67–68, 72, 104, 117
marriage, xvii, 31–32, 34, 86, 91, 108
margin/s, xvi, xviii, 8, 38, 43–46, 63, 75, 120
marginalization/marginalized, xiii, xiv, xix, 12, 13, 15, 19, 25, 36, 38, 48, 57, 61, 79, 81–84, 89, 93, 95, 103, 114, 118
Martinez, Elizabeth, 7
matrix of domination, xiv, xviii, 5–7, 92, 93, 107, 115
May, Vivian, xiii, xvi, 3–4, 7, 13–15, 20, 43, 65, 84, 113, 121
McDougall, Joy, 50
meritocracy, 9
mestiza, 6
middle class, 10, 20, 22, 26, 72, 82
Middle Collegiate Church, 97
minjung, xiii, 36, 44, 64, 115
ministry, xvii, 26–30, 86–88, 96, 99–101, 103, 105–6, 120
Mitchem, Stephanie, 45–46, 121
misogyny, 86, 95
Moraga, Cherrie, 20
multiplicity, xii, 12, 37, 44, 46, 65, 67–68, 77, 88–89, 95, 107
mujerista, xiii, 38, 42, 45, 64, 115

Nadar, Sarojini, 74
nation, xi, xviii, 9, 18–19, 31, 34, 38, 41, 45–46, 49, 52, 60, 72, 86–87, 92, 98, 102, 113–14, 117–18
Native American, xvii, 42, 52–53

Oduyoye, Mercy, 51, 54, 91, 121
oppression, ix, xi, xiii–xix, 2, 4–9, 11–14, 17, 19, 36, 38, 41, 45–47, 55, 62, 68, 70, 72, 75–76, 79, 82, 84, 89–90, 93–95, 108–9, 111, 113–118
ordination, xiii, xiv, xvii, 6, 13, 15, 18, 28, 30–32, 46, 51, 57, 70, 80, 89, 101–4, 113
Ostriker, Alicia Suskin, 42
other, xi, xii, xiv, xvi–xviii, 2, 3, 5–9, 11–14, 18–20, 22–23, 25, 31–35, 37–39, 41, 43, 45–48, 50, 52, 54, 59, 64, 68–72, 74–75, 79–80, 82, 84–86, 89–91, 101–4, 107, 109–10, 113–14, 117–18, 120

patriarchy/patriarchal, xii, xviii, 24–25, 29, 31, 32, 36–37, 48, 50, 52, 55, 57, 60, 64, 72, 75–76, 82, 103–4
peace, xix, 16, 25, 45, 82, 88, 96, 105, 108, 110
Pentateuch, 75
Philo, 66
Plato, 65
Pneumatology, 61, 68–70, 77
postcolonial, xi, 38, 42, 46–47, 62, 64, 70–72, 74, 88–90, 114, 116, 121
poverty, 13, 38, 47, 51–52, 70–71, 98–99, 115, 118, 124
praxis, xiv, xviii, 2, 42, 43, 55, 57, 58, 80–81, 89, 94, 116

prayer, 25, 70, 72, 81, 86–87, 97, 100, 104
priesthood of believers, 103
privilege, xii, xvii, xviii, 2, 5, 8, 10–12, 20–21, 27, 34, 44–45, 47, 49, 60, 73, 76, 79, 80, 83, 84, 87, 103, 107–9
Process Theology, xii, 36–38, 40, 116
prophetic, xvi, 52, 86, 94
Protestant, 5

queer, xi, xiii, xv, xvii, 13, 16, 35, 42, 44–46, 57, 59, 64, 68, 72–74, 81, 114, 117, 121–22
queer theology, 16, 45, 59, 68, 73, 117, 121

race, xi, xiii–xv, xvii–xviii, 1, 2, 4–11, 13–16, 18–19, 34–35, 38, 41, 44–46, 48–49, 52–54, 58, 60, 63, 68, 71–74, 76, 80–81, 85–88, 90–92, 98–99, 102, 108, 110, 113–18, 121–22
racism, xvii, xix, 4–5, 10, 22–23, 25, 27–30, 35–36, 38, 45, 47, 59, 64, 71, 75, 79–80, 82, 86, 95, 114–17
Reformation Project, 99
religion/religious, xi, xvi, 2, 6, 10, 18–19, 27–28, 34, 36, 38, 42, 46–50, 52, 54, 56, 61, 68–70, 73–76, 85–86, 89–91, 95, 98, 105, 107–10, 113, 115–18
resistance, xvi, xviii, 7–8, 10, 12, 47, 51–52, 55, 63–64, 90–91, 95, 117
resurrection, 56, 95
Ruether, Rosemary Radford, 44
Russell, Letty, 44
Ruth and Naomi, xviii, 73

sacraments, 100–103
Samaritan woman at the well, 74
Sarah, 32, 71
segregation, xiv, 86, 90, 93
sexism, xvii, xix, 4–5, 10, 20, 25, 27, 35, 38, 45, 60, 71, 79–80, 95, 114–17
sexual identity/sexuality, v, xi, xiii, xv, xvii–xviii, 2–3, 5–7, 9, 11, 13–14, 18–19, 35, 38, 41, 44–49, 54, 60, 68, 73–76, 80–81, 85–87, 92–93, 98–99, 108–10, 113–14, 117–20
simultaneous/simultaneity, xi, 2, 5, 7–9, 19, 44–45, 68, 83, 88, 109, 115
single-axis, xiii, 3, 7, 8, 10, 13, 53, 64, 68, 90, 92, 95, 108, 117
slavery, xiv, 30, 75, 82, 86, 90, 93
slippages, 8, 10, 64, 117
Smith, Beverly, 6, 126
Smith, Barbara, 6, 8, 121
social justice, xiv, 2, 10, 12, 17, 18, 61, 80, 97, 107, 117
social location, xi, xii, xiv, xviii, 2–3, 11, 13–14, 17–18, 20–21, 41, 44–45, 49, 51–52, 54, 60, 70–73, 77, 80, 83, 91–92, 107–9, 117
Song, Cathy, 6
Sophia, xi, 42, 54, 67–68, 77, 120
Southern Baptist, xvii, 26–29, 49
spirituality, 48, 61, 82, 106
status quo, 55, 59, 64, 70, 76, 88, 98
subjugation, xix, 38
Sugirtharajah, R. S., 46, 47
suffering, 10, 37
syncretism, 54, 89

text of terror, 73

theological method, vii, xvii, 16, 41, 43, 46, 48, 51, 76, 96, 110
theology of indeterminacy, 42
Thomas, Linda, 61
transformation, 2, 7, 52, 56, 88, 95, 99, 103–5, 110
transgender/trans, xviii, 53, 56, 60, 73, 82, 118–19
Trible, Phyllis, 73, 121
Truth, Sojourner, 4
Tsui, Kitty, 6
two-thirds world, 86, 93, 110, 118

Wang, Lily Kuo, 103
Watson, Natalie K., 89–91, 100, 103, 122
Wells, Ida B., 1, 4
West, Mona, 73–74, 120
white privilege, 27, 116
white supremacy, 25, 59, 82, 86

whiteness, xiv, 14, 59, 72, 104
Williams, Delores S., ix, xviii, 45, 71, 91, 96, 122
Wilson, Nancy, 73, 122
wisdom, ix, 54, 67
womanist, xiii, 4, 6, 12–13, 16, 38, 42, 45, 61, 64, 70–71, 73–74, 81, 91, 96, 119, 121–22
women, black, xii, xvii, 1, 2–6, 16, 48, 61, 91, 96, 118
women of color, xvi, xvii, 3, 6, 44, 47, 53, 80, 81, 90, 109, 118
women, white, 1–4, 47, 49, 81, 116
Woodley, Randy, 52, 122
Worship, xiii, 28, 75, 84, 87, 96–97, 100, 104–5

xenophobia, 95, 118

Young, Robert, 87, 114, 122

www.ingramcontent.com/pod-product-compliance
Ingram Content Group UK Ltd.
Pitfield, Milton Keynes, MK11 3LW, UK
UKHW021326180426
11947UKWH00017B/1465